How to Talk to Anyone
Connect & Conquer

Ed Merid

Table of Contents

Introduction 1

Chapter 1: The First Connection 3

  1.1: The Science of First Impressions 4

    1.1.1 : What happens in the brain during first impressions 5

    1.1.2 : How to make a lasting, positive impact 6

  1.2 : Crafting Your Introduction 8

    1.2.1 : Step-by-step guide to introducing yourself in different contexts 8

    1.2.2: Key do's and don'ts 10

Chapter 2: The Art of Conversation 12

  2.1: Mastering Small Talk 13

    2.1.1 : Techniques to move beyond surface-level conversation 13

    2.1.2 : Asking the right questions to deepen a connection 16

  2.2: Active Listening and Empathy 19

    2.2.1: The art of listening to respond, not just to speak 20

    2.2.2 - Using empathy to create stronger bonds 22

Chapter 3: Non-Verbal Communication and Body Language 26

  3.1: Decoding Gestures and Body Language 27

    3.1.1: How to interpret others' body language 28

    3.1.2 : Adjusting your own non-verbal cues for better communication 30

  3.2: The Impact of Eye Contact and Space 33

    3.2.1 : The psychology behind eye contact 34

    3.2.2 : Understanding personal space across different cultures 36

Chapter 4: Storytelling and Persuasion 41

  4.1: Crafting Your Narrative 42

4.1.1 : How to tell a story that captivates and persuades......... 43

4.1.2 : Structuring stories for maximum impact..................... 46

4.2: The Power of Stories in Business and Life 50

4.2.1: Why storytelling is essential for influence? 52

4.2.2: Real-life examples of successful storytelling.................. 55

Chapter 5: Navigating Challenging Communication Scenarios 58

5.1: Strategies for Difficult Conversations................................ 60

5.1.1: How to keep calm and maintain control in tense situations? 61

5.1.2 : Defusing arguments without sacrificing your point...... 64

5.2: Overcoming Communication Anxiety 68

5.2.1 : Techniques to manage social and public speaking anxiety 69

5.2.2: Building confidence in conversations 72

Chapter 6: Digital and Cross-Cultural Communication 77

6.1: Mastering Digital Communication 78

6.1.1 : Email etiquette and social media best practices 79

6.1.2 : Building rapport in virtual meetings and online networking 83

6.2: Cross-Cultural Communication.. 88

6.2.1 : Understanding cultural communication styles 89

6.2.2 : Building Global Relationships and Avoiding Cultural Missteps 93

Chapter 7: Advanced Communication Skills 100

7.1: Emotional Intelligence in Communication........................ 101

7.1.1 : Recognizing and managing emotions in yourself and others 102

7.1.2: Adapting to different communication styles 107

7.2: The Ethics of Communication... 111

7.2.1: Honesty and integrity in communication..................... 112

7.2.2: Responsible use of persuasion techniques................... 116

Chapter 8: The Future of Communication 121

8.1: Embracing Technological Changes 122

8.1.1 : How AI and automation are reshaping communication
.... 123

8.2: Predicting Communication Trends 129

8.2.1: Future trends in work and social communication 131

**8.2.2 :Preparing for the next wave of digital communication
tools**.. 134

Conclusion.. 139

Introduction

Picture this: You're standing at the edge of a crowded room. The air buzzes with conversation, laughter, and the clink of glasses. Your palms are sweaty, your heart races. "How do they do it?" you wonder, watching others effortlessly flit from group to group, leaving smiles and nods in their wake. If this scenario makes your stomach churn, you're not alone. But what if I told you that this fear, this paralyzing anxiety of human interaction, could become your greatest strength?

"How to Talk to Anyone: Connect & Conquer" isn't just a book. It's a revolution disguised as 200-odd pages of paper and ink. It's the key to unlocking a superpower you never knew you had.

Think about it. In a world where we swipe right for love and click 'like' for friendship, the art of real, face-to-face connection has become a rare and valuable commodity. Those who master it? They're the ones who land the jobs, win the deals, and yes, get the girl (or guy).

But here's the kicker, this isn't about becoming some smooth-talking, manipulative chameleon. God knows we've got enough of those. No, this is about something far more powerful: becoming authentically, unapologetically you, and learning how to share that self with the world.

From dissecting the science of first impressions (did you know it takes just 7 seconds to make one?) to unraveling the mystery of body language, we're going to dive deep into the nitty-gritty of human connection. We'll explore why some stories captivate while others bore, and how a single well-placed question can transform a stilted exchange into a life-changing conversation.

You'll learn to navigate the treacherous waters of small talk, turning those dreaded "Nice weather we're having" moments into launchpads for genuine connection.

We'll tackle the digital frontier too, because let's face it in 2024, knowing how to craft a killer email is just as important as knowing how to work a room.

So, who's this book for? The shy introvert longing to break free from their shell? Absolutely. The seasoned networker looking to fine-tune their skills? You bet. The average Joe or Jane who simply wants to make their daily interactions a little less awkward and a lot more meaningful? This is your bible.

Because here's the truth: in a world obsessed with followers and likes, real connection is the ultimate currency. And by the time you finish this book, you'll be rich beyond your wildest dreams.

Ready to connect and conquer? Let's talk.

Chapter 1: The First Connection

The clock ticks. Your heart races. In just moments, you'll step into a room that could change your life. A job interview? A first date? A high-stakes business meeting? It doesn't matter. What matters is this: you have seconds, mere seconds, to make an impression that could last a lifetime.

Terrifying, isn't it?

But what if I told you that those fleeting moments aren't just manageable, but conquerable? That's right. The power to captivate, to intrigue, to connect, it's all within your grasp. And it starts here, with the first connection.

Let's cut through the noise. We're all familiar with the clichés about first impressions. But here's what they don't tell you: the game is rigged from the start. Your brain, that magnificent organ nestled in your skull, makes snap judgments faster than you can blink. It's an evolutionary hangover, a relic from when quickly sizing up friend or foe meant the difference between life and death.

Today, that same split-second assessment could mean the difference between landing your dream job or watching it slip away. Between sparking a romance or facing another lonely night. Between sealing a deal or watching it evaporate before your eyes.

So, how do we hack this system? How do we ensure that when someone's brain performs that lightning-fast calculation, we come out on top?

It's not about grand gestures or rehearsed speeches. It's about understanding the subtle dance of human interaction. It's about recognizing that while your words matter, they're only a small part of the story you're telling.

Your body language communicates powerfully before you even say a word. The tilt of your head, the set of your shoulders, the way you occupy space, all of these send powerful signals. And your voice? It's not only what you say, but how you say it. The pitch, the pace, the timbre, each element paints a picture of who you are.

But here's where it gets fascinating. These aren't just arbitrary signals. They're deeply rooted in our psychology, tied to primal instincts of trust, competence, and likability. Master these, and you've got the key to unlocking instant rapport with almost anyone.

Throughout this chapter, we'll delve into the nitty-gritty of crafting that perfect first impression. You'll learn how to read a room like a pro, how to adjust your approach on the fly, and how to leave people thinking, "Wow, who was that?"

We'll explore real-world scenarios, breaking down successful (and not-so-successful) first encounters. You'll discover how tiny tweaks in your approach can yield massive results. And you'll gain the confidence to walk into any situation knowing you can connect with anyone.

Remember, this isn't about becoming someone you're not. It's about highlighting the best aspects of who you are. It's about giving yourself the best possible chance to connect, to succeed, to thrive.

By the time we're done, you'll see every new encounter as an opportunity, not a challenge. You'll have the tools to turn strangers into allies, acquaintances into friends, and fleeting moments into lasting connections.

So, are you ready to unlock the secrets of the first connection? To harness the power of those crucial first moments? To transform the way you interact with the world?

Let's begin. Your journey to mastering the art of the first impression starts now. And trust me, it's going to be one hell of a ride.

1.1: The Science of First Impressions

First impressions are like the opening scene of a movie – they set the tone for everything that follows. But what's really going on beneath the surface during these crucial moments? Let's dive into the fascinating world of first impressions and uncover the science that drives them.

When we meet someone new, our brains kick into high gear, processing a wealth of information in mere seconds. This rapid-fire analysis involves multiple brain regions working in concert to form an initial judgment. The amygdala, our emotional center, quickly assesses potential threats or rewards. Meanwhile, the fusiform face area analyzes facial features, and the prefrontal cortex begins creating higher-level judgments.

Interestingly, research has shown that these split-second evaluations often focus on two key factors: warmth and competence. Warmth relates to how friendly, trustworthy, and kind someone appears, while competence assesses their perceived ability and skill level. These two dimensions constitute the backbone of our social perceptions, influencing how we interact with others from the very first moment.

But why do our brains work this way? From an evolutionary perspective, quick assessments of others' intentions (warmth) and abilities (competence) were crucial for survival. In today's world, these rapid judgments continue to shape our social interactions, influencing everything from job interviews to romantic encounters.

Understanding this process isn't just academically fascinating, it's practically useful. By recognizing how our brains form first impressions, we can better navigate social situations and consciously shape the impressions we make on others. This knowledge empowers us to build stronger connections and more meaningful relationships from the very first hello.

1.1.1 : What happens in the brain during first impressions

Picture this: you walk into a room for a job interview. Your palms are sweaty, your heart is racing, and you're desperately trying to remember everything you've rehearsed. But before you even open your mouth, your interviewer's brain is already hard at work, creating an impression of you.

In the blink of an eye – literally less than a second – several key areas of the brain spring into action. Our emotional regulator, the amygdala, twinkles like a Christmas tree. This almond-shaped structure is responsible for processing social cues and potential threats, making it a crucial player in first impressions.

Meanwhile, the fusiform face area, a region specialized in facial recognition, begins analyzing your features. It's looking for familiar patterns and comparing them to a vast database of faces and associated memories.

But here's where it gets fascinating: as these areas process raw data, the prefrontal cortex – the brain's CEO – starts making judgments. And it does so based on two primary factors: warmth and competence.

Warmth relates to how friendly, trustworthy, and kind you seem. Competence, on the other hand, is about how capable and intelligent you appear. These two factors form the backbone of almost every first impression.

Let's consider Sarah, a marketing executive. When she walks into a client meeting, she makes sure to smile warmly (signaling warmth) while standing tall with confident posture (indicating competence). Without realizing it, she's giving the client's brain exactly what it needs to create a positive first impression.

1.1.2 : How to make a lasting, positive impact

Now that we understand what's happening in the brain, how can we use this knowledge to our advantage? The key lies in consciously projecting both warmth and competence in those crucial first moments.

Start with your body language. Research shows that adopting a "power pose" – standing tall with your shoulders back and your hands on your hips – for just two minutes before an important interaction can significantly boost your confidence. This increased self-assurance translates into more competent body language during the actual encounter.

Next, focus on your facial expressions. A genuine smile is one of the most powerful tools in your first impression arsenal. It signals warmth and approachability, making others more likely to respond positively to you.

Consider the case of Alex, an introverted software developer who always struggled in networking events. After learning about the science of first impressions, he made a conscious effort to smile more and maintain open body language. The results were remarkable – he found people approaching him more often and conversations flowing more easily.

But it's not just about non-verbal cues. The words you choose in those initial moments matter too. Using the other person's name, showing genuine interest in what they're saying, and finding common ground can all help establish a connection quickly.

Remember James, a sales representative who always seemed to close deals effortlessly? His secret was simple – he always started conversations by finding a shared interest with his clients. This approach tapped into the brain's tendency to favor people who seem similar to us, creating an instant rapport.

As we wrap up this exploration of first impressions, it's important to remember that while these initial judgments happen quickly, they're not set in stone. Our brains are remarkably adaptable, capable of updating impressions with new information. This means that even if a first impression doesn't go as planned, all is not lost. Consistency in your actions and genuine interactions can help reshape perceptions over time.

Practical Exercise:

Before your next essential first encounter, try this exercise. Stand in front of a mirror and practice your "power pose" for two minutes. Then, smile genuinely and introduce yourself as if meeting someone for the first time. Pay attention to your body language, tone of voice, and the words you choose. How do you come across? Does your presentation balance warmth and competence? Make adjustments until you feel you're projecting the best version of yourself. After that, go out and use it in real life. The favorable reactions you get may surprise you.

By understanding and applying the science of first impressions, you're not just improving your chances of making a good impression, you're opening doors to richer, more meaningful connections in all areas of your life.

1.2 : Crafting Your Introduction

You've made it through the initial moments of a first impression, but now comes a crucial step: introducing yourself. This seemingly simple act can be a powerful tool in shaping how others perceive you, whether you're at a job interview, a networking event, or a social gathering.

A well-crafted introduction is your opportunity to showcase both warmth and competence, the two key factors in forming positive impressions. It's your chance to present yourself authentically while highlighting your best qualities.

In this subchapter, we'll explore the art and science of introductions. We'll provide a step-by-step guide to introducing yourself effectively in various contexts, and we'll discuss the key do's and don'ts that can make or break your introduction.

By mastering the skill of self-introduction, you'll be equipped to navigate any social or professional situation with confidence. Let's dive in and discover how to make your introduction a compelling opening act that leaves your audience eager for more.

1.2.1 : Step-by-step guide to introducing yourself in different contexts

Introducing yourself effectively is a skill that can open doors in both personal and professional settings. Let's explore how to craft compelling introductions for various scenarios.

1. Professional Networking Events:

Step 1: Start with a warm smile and confident body language.

Step 2: Offer a firm handshake (where culturally appropriate).

Step 3: State your name clearly.

Step 4: Share your professional role and company.

Step 5: Add a brief, unique detail about your work or interests.

Example: "Hi, I'm Sarah Chen. I'm a software engineer at TechInnovate. I specialize in AI applications that are making waves in healthcare."

2. Job Interviews:

Step 1: Maintain eye contact and offer a friendly smile.

Step 2: Use the interviewer's name if you know it.

Step 3: State your name and express gratitude for the opportunity.

Step 4: Provide a brief overview of your relevant experience.

Step 5: Express enthusiasm for the role.

Example: "Good morning, Ms. Thompson. I'm Alex Rodriguez. I appreciate you coming in to see me today. I've been working in digital marketing for five years, specializing in social media strategy. Furthermore, I'm really excited about the possibility of bringing my experience to your innovative team."

3. Social Gatherings:

Step 1: Approach with open body language and a genuine smile.

Step 2: Offer a warm greeting.

Step 3: State your name.

Step 4: Mention how you're connected to the event or host.

Step 5: Ask an open-ended question to start a conversation.

Example: "Hi there! I'm Michael. I'm a friend of the host, Emma, from college. This is a great party, isn't it? What's your connection to Emma?"

Remember, the key is to balance warmth (through your smile, tone, and friendly demeanor) with competence (by highlighting relevant skills or experiences). Tailor your introduction to the context, keeping it concise yet engaging.

1.2.2: Key do's and don'ts

To ensure your introductions make the best possible impression, keep these crucial do's and don'ts in mind:

Do's:

1. Do maintain eye contact: This shows confidence and engagement.

2. Do smile genuinely: A warm smile can instantly make others feel at ease.

3. Do listen actively: Show interest in others' responses to build rapport.

4. Do practice your introduction: Rehearsing can help you feel more confident.

5. Do be authentic: Let your personality shine through.

Don'ts:

1. Don't ramble: Keep your introduction concise and to the point.

2. Don't use jargon: Ensure your language is accessible to everyone.

3. Don't forget names: Try to remember and use others' names in conversation.

4. Don't interrupt: Wait for a natural pause before introducing yourself in group settings.

5. Don't oversell: Be confident but avoid coming across as boastful.

Case Study: The Influence of a Strong Introduction

Meet Tom, a graphic designer attending his first major industry conference. Initially nervous, Tom prepared a concise introduction, highlighting both his skills and his passion for design. When he met the CEO of a company he admired, Tom confidently said:

"Hello, I'm Tom Carter. I'm a graphic designer specializing in eco-friendly packaging design. Your company's commitment to sustainability has been a huge inspiration for my work. I'd love to hear more about your latest projects."

This introduction showcased Tom's competence (his specialization) and warmth (his genuine interest in the company). It led to an engaging conversation and eventually, a job offer.

Practical Exercise:

Craft three versions of your introduction for different contexts: professional, casual, and a wildcard scenario of your choice. Practice these in front of a mirror or with a friend. Pay attention to your body language and tone. After each practice run, reflect on what felt natural and what needs improvement. Remember, the goal is to feel comfortable and authentic while effectively communicating who you are.

By mastering the art of introduction, you're not just sharing your name – you're opening the door to meaningful connections and exciting opportunities. With practice and authenticity, you'll be able to make a lasting, positive impression in any situation.

Chapter 2: The Art of Conversation

Ever watched in awe as someone effortlessly charms a room, their words weaving a tapestry of engagement and connection? That's the power of masterful conversation – a skill that can transform ordinary interactions into extraordinary experiences.

Conversation is the heartbeat of human interaction, pulsing with the potential to forge bonds, spark ideas, and open doors to new opportunities. Yet, for many, the art of dialogue remains an enigmatic challenge, often fraught with anxiety and uncertainty.

This chapter aims to demystify the secrets of engaging conversation, equipping you with the tools to become a verbal virtuoso. We'll explore how to strike the perfect balance between warmth and competence in your exchanges, ensuring your words not only inform but also captivate.

Our journey will take us through the full spectrum of conversational scenarios, from breaking the ice to navigating sensitive topics. You'll discover the power of active listening, learn to speak compellingly, and uncover the subtle cues that typically go unnoticed. We'll delve into the psychology behind great conversations, uncovering why some discussions flourish while others falter.

As we progress, you'll come to realize that great conversation isn't about having all the answers or dominating the dialogue. It's about curiosity, empathy, and the ability to gracefully alternate between speaking and listening. It's an art form that, when mastered, can elevate every interaction into an opportunity for growth, understanding, and genuine human connection.

By the end of this chapter, you'll be prepared to craft words like a master, transforming even the most routine encounters into memorable exchanges. So, let's embark on this verbal voyage and unlock the true potential of artful conversation.

2.1: Mastering Small Talk

Small talk: the social lubricant that often gets a bad rap. Many dismiss it as trivial, yet it's the gateway to deeper connections and opportunities. In this subchapter, we'll unveil the hidden power of those seemingly insignificant exchanges and transform your approach to everyday conversations.

Think of small talk as the appetizer of social interaction. It whets the appetite for more substantial dialogue, setting the stage for meaningful connections. By mastering this art, you'll navigate social waters with ease, whether you're at a networking event, a family gathering, or chatting with a stranger in line for coffee.

We'll explore how to strike the perfect balance between warmth and competence in your small talk repertoire. You'll learn to exude friendliness while showcasing your social savvy, making every interaction count.

This section will equip you with practical techniques to elevate your conversational game. We'll delve into strategies for moving beyond weather chat and into engaging territory. You'll discover the power of asking the right questions, turning small talk into big opportunities for connection.

By the time you finish this subchapter, you'll view small talk not as a necessary evil, but as a powerful tool in your social toolkit. You'll be ready to turn those brief encounters into memorable exchanges, opening doors to new relationships and opportunities.

Let's dive in and uncover the secrets to making every word count, no matter how small the talk may seem.

2.1.1 : Techniques to move beyond surface-level conversation

Small talk doesn't have to be small in impact. With the right techniques, you can transform seemingly trivial exchanges into gateways for deeper connection.

Here's how to elevate your conversational game:

1. The art of active listening

Active listening is the cornerstone of meaningful conversation. Understanding the speaker's message and feelings is more important than only hearing what they have to say. When you truly listen, you pick up on subtle cues that can guide the conversation to more interesting places.

Technique: The Echo Method

Try repeating key phrases or ideas back to the speaker, but in your own words. This shows you're engaged and provides an opportunity to dig deeper.

Example:

Speaker: "I've been so busy with work lately."

You: "It sounds like your job has been asking a lot of your time. What's been keeping you so occupied?"

2. Finding common ground

Discovering shared interests or experiences can quickly move a conversation beyond surface level. It creates a sense of connection and provides rich material for further discussion.

Technique: The Interest of Detective

Listen for clues about the person's interests, then explore those topics further.

Example:

Speaker: "I'm looking forward to the weekend. If the weather is nice, I might go hiking."

You: "Oh, you enjoy hiking? I love outdoor activities too. What's your favorite trail around here?"

3. Sharing personal anecdotes

Offering a brief, relevant personal story can add depth to the conversation and encourage the other person to open up as well. The key is to keep it concise and relatable.

Technique: The Story Spark

Share a short, engaging anecdote related to the current topic, then pivot back to the other person.

Example:

You: "Speaking of hiking, I once got lost on a trail and ended up stumbling upon the most beautiful hidden waterfall. Have you ever had any unexpected discoveries on your hikes?"

4. Using open-ended questions

Closed questions that can be answered with a simple "yes" or "no" often lead to conversational dead ends. Open-ended questions, on the other hand, invite elaboration and keep the dialogue flowing.

Technique: The Curiosity Catalyst

Frame your questions to encourage detailed responses.

Example:

Instead of: "Did you have a good weekend?"

Try: "What was the highlight of your weekend?"

5. Embracing the power of silence

Many people rush to fill silence, frequently with the first thing that comes to mind. However, comfortable silences can lead to more thoughtful responses and deeper conversations.

Technique: The Thoughtful Pause

Allow a little period of pause after posing a question. This gives the other person time to reflect and frequently leads to more meaningful answers.

2.1.2 : Asking the right questions to deepen a connection

The questions you ask can make or break a conversation. By asking the right questions, you demonstrate both warmth (showing genuine interest) and competence (asking insightful questions).

Here's how to master the art of questioning:

1. The funnel approach

Begin with more general inquiries and work your way down to more focused ones. This approach helps you gauge the other person's comfort level and interest in various topics.

Example:

Broad: "What do you enjoy doing in your free time?"

Narrower: "You mentioned you like reading. What genre do you prefer?"

Specific: "What was the last book that really impacted you, and why?"

2. Follow-up questions

Don't just move from one question to the next. Show genuine interest in asking follow-up questions based on the answers you receive.

Example:

Initial question: "What do you do for work?"

Follow-up: "That sounds interesting. What drew you to that field?"

Deeper follow-up: "What's been your biggest challenge in that role, and how have you tackled it?"

3. Emotion-based questions

Questions that tap into emotions can quickly deepen a connection. They show empathy and invite the other person to share more personal insights.

Example:

"What's been the most exciting part of your job lately?"

"When was the last time you felt really proud of something you accomplished?"

4. Value-based questions

These questions help you understand the other person's core values and beliefs, fostering a deeper connection.

Example:

"What's one thing you wish you could change about the world?"

"Who has been the biggest influence in your life, and why?"

5. Hypothetical questions

These can be fun and revealing, encouraging creative thinking and providing insights into the person's personality.

Example:

"If you could have dinner with any historical figure, who would it be and why?"

"If you could master any skill instantly, which one would you pick?"

6. Story-eliciting questions

Everyone has stories to tell. The right questions can bring these stories to the surface, making for engaging conversation.

Example:

"What's the most adventurous thing you've ever done?"

"Can you tell me about a time when you overcame a significant challenge?"

Case Study: The Networking Event Turnaround

Sarah, an introverted software developer, always dreaded networking events. She would often find herself stuck in awkward silences or trapped in dull conversations about the weather. After learning these techniques, she decided to put them into practice at her next industry meetup.

As she approached a group, instead of her usual "How's it going?", she opened with, "I just heard an interesting talk on AI ethics. What are your thoughts on the ethical implications of AI in our industry?"

This question showcased her competence (knowledge of industry trends) while inviting others to share their opinions. It sparked a lively discussion, allowing Sarah to use active listening techniques and ask follow-up questions.

When the conversation turned to career paths, Sarah used the funnel approach:

Broad: "How did you all get into tech?"

Narrower: "What has been the most unexpected part of your career journey?"

Specific: "Can you describe a moment that made you realize you were on the right track?"

By the end of the event, Sarah had made several meaningful connections and even landed a coffee meeting with a potential mentor. She left feeling energized rather than drained, all thanks to her new conversational skills.

Practical Exercise: The Question Challenge

For the next week, challenge yourself to ask at least one meaningful question in every conversation you have. Keep a journal of the questions you ask and the responses they elicit. Notice how different types of questions affect the flow and depth of your conversations.

At the end of the week, reflect on your experiences:

- Which questions led to the most engaging conversations?
- Did you notice any patterns in how people responded to different types of questions?
- How did asking these questions make you feel? Did it change your perception of small talk?

Remember, mastering the art of conversation is a journey, not a destination. Every interaction offers a chance to practice and improve your skills. With time and practice, you'll find yourself moving effortlessly from small talk to meaningful dialogue, creating connections that last long after the conversation ends.

2.2: Active Listening and Empathy

In the symphony of conversation, active listening and empathy are the harmonious notes that create a masterpiece of human connection. These skills form the bedrock of meaningful dialogue, transforming superficial exchanges into profound interactions.

Active listening goes beyond merely hearing words; it's about fully engaging with the speaker, understanding their message, and responding thoughtfully. It's a powerful tool that demonstrates both warmth and competence in your interactions. By actively listening, you show that you value the other person's thoughts and feelings, creating an atmosphere of trust and openness.

Empathy, however, is the capacity to understand and connect with another person's emotions. It's the emotional bridge that connects us to others, allowing us to see the world through their eyes. When combined with active listening, empathy becomes a potent force for building stronger, more authentic relationships.

In this subchapter, we'll explore the art of listening to respond, not just to speak. You'll learn techniques to become a more attentive listener, picking up on subtle cues and unspoken messages. We'll also delve into the power of empathy and how it can be used to create deeper, more meaningful connections in both personal and professional settings.

By mastering these skills, you'll elevate your conversational abilities to new heights. You'll become the person others seek out for meaningful dialogue, the colleague known for insightful contributions, and the friend valued for genuine understanding. Let's embark on this journey to unlock the full potential of active listening and empathy in your interactions.

2.2.1: The art of listening to respond, not just to speak

Many people listen with the intent to reply, their minds already formulating responses before the speaker has finished. True active listening, however, involves fully focusing on the speaker, understanding their message, and responding thoughtfully. Here's how to master this art:

1. Give your full attention

The initial step in active listening is to be completely present. Set aside distractions and concentrate fully on the speaker.

Technique: The Presence Practice

Before entering a conversation, take a deep breath and mentally set aside your own thoughts and concerns. Imagine creating a clear, open space in your mind to receive the speaker's words.

2. Use non-verbal cues

Your body language speaks volumes. Use it to show you're engaged and attentive.

Technique: The Mirror Method

Subtly mirror the speaker's body language. If they lean in, lean in slightly. If they speak softly, lower your voice. This creates a sense of rapport and shows you're in sync.

3. Practice reflective listening

Reflect back what you've heard to ensure understanding and show you're paying attention.

Technique: The Paraphrase Pause

After the speaker makes a point, pause briefly, then paraphrase what you've heard. For example, "So what I'm hearing is..."

4. Ask clarifying questions

Don't assume you understand everything. Ask questions to clarify points and show your interest.

Technique: The Curious Questioner

Prepare a mental list of open-ended questions like "Can you tell me more about that?" or "How did that make you feel?"

5. Avoid interrupting

Wait till the other person has finished speaking before responding. Interrupting can break the flow of the conversation and make the speaker feel ignored.

Technique: The Patience Pause

If you feel the urge to interject, take a deep breath and count to three. This gives you a moment to reconsider and often allows the speaker to continue naturally.

Empathy is the ability to understand and share the feelings of another. It's a powerful tool for creating deeper connections and fostering understanding. Here's how to cultivate and use empathy effectively:

1. Practice perspective-taking

Make an effort to understand the situation from the other person's perspective, even if you don't agree.

Technique: The Empathy Swap

Imagine swapping places with the speaker. How would you feel in their situation? What would your concerns be?

2. Validate emotions

Acknowledge the speaker's feelings, even if you can't fully relate to them.

Technique: The Feeling Finder

Listen for emotional cues in the speaker's words and tone. Respond with phrases like, "That must have been difficult," or "I can understand why you'd feel that way."

3. Share similar experiences

If appropriate, share your own experiences that relate to the speaker's situation. This can foster a sense of mutual understanding.

Technique: The Connective Anecdote

Briefly share a similar experience, then quickly return the focus to the speaker. For example, "I've felt that way before. How are you handling it?"

4. Use empathetic language

Choose words that show understanding and support.

Technique: The Compassion Vocabulary

Build a repertoire of empathetic phrases like "I'm here for you," "That sounds challenging," or "Your feelings are valid."

5. Practice active empathy

Go beyond understanding to taking supportive action.

Technique: The Empathy Action

Ask, "How can I support you?" or "What do you need right now?" Then follow through on what they express.

Case Study: The Team Leader's Transformation

Mark, a tech startup team leader, was known for his brilliant ideas but poor interpersonal skills. His team felt unheard and undervalued, leading to low morale and high turnover. After attending a workshop on active listening and empathy, Mark decided to change his approach.

In his next team meeting, instead of dominating the conversation, Mark practiced active listening. When a team member, Sarah, expressed frustration with a project, Mark used the Paraphrase Pause technique:

Mark: "So, if I understand correctly, you're feeling overwhelmed by the project timeline and worried about meeting the deadline. Is that right?"

Sarah nodded, surprised by Mark's attentiveness. Mark then employed the Empathy Action technique:

Mark: "That sounds really stressful. How can I support you in managing this workload?"

This simple exchange had a profound effect. Sarah felt heard and valued, and together they worked out a solution to redistribute some tasks. Over the next few months, as Mark consistently applied these techniques, team morale improved dramatically. Communication became more open, problem-solving more collaborative, and team members reported feeling more valued and understood.

By the end of the quarter, not only had turnover decreased, but the team's productivity had increased by 30%. Mark's transformation from a task-focused leader to an empathetic, active listener had created a more positive and productive work environment.

Practical Exercise: The Empathy Journal

For one week, keep an "Empathy Journal." Each day, record at least one interaction where you practiced active listening and empathy. Write down:

1. What was the situation?

2. What active listening techniques did you use?

3. How did you demonstrate empathy?

4. How did the other person respond?

5. What did you learn from this interaction?

At the week's end, take some time to review your journal. Reflect on how these practices affected your conversations and relationships. Did you notice any changes in how people responded to you? Did you feel any differently about your interactions?

Remember, mastering active listening and empathy is an ongoing process. Every conversation presents a chance to practice and enhance your skills. As you continue to hone these skills, you'll likely find your relationships deepening, your understanding of others growing, and your own emotional intelligence expanding.

By combining the power of active listening with the warmth of empathy, you create a conversational approach that is both competent and caring. This powerful combination will not only enhance your personal relationships but can also lead to greater success in professional settings, making you a more effective communicator, leader, and collaborator.

Chapter 3: Non-Verbal Communication and Body Language

Words may be the stars of the communication show, but non-verbal cues and body language are the unsung heroes that truly steal the scene. In this chapter, we'll pull back the curtain on the silent symphony that plays alongside our spoken words, revealing the powerful impact of gestures, facial expressions, and posture on our daily interactions.

Approximately 93% of communication is nonverbal. Did you realize that? That's right, while we focus on crafting the perfect phrase, our bodies are busy telling stories of their own. Mastering the art of non-verbal communication is like learning a universal language, one that transcends cultural barriers and speaks directly to our instincts.

We'll explore how to harness the dual forces of warmth and competence through your physical presence. You'll discover how to project confidence without appearing arrogant, and how to convey empathy without seeming weak. This delicate balance is the key to making lasting impressions and building trust in both personal and professional spheres.

From the subtleties of eye contact to the nuances of personal space, we'll decode the secret signals that can make or break a conversation. You'll learn to read others like an open book, picking up on hidden emotions and unspoken messages. More importantly, you'll gain control over your own non-verbal cues, ensuring that your body aligns with your words to deliver a cohesive and compelling message.

Get ready to embark on a fascinating journey through the world of silent communication. By the time you finish this chapter, you'll view every interaction through a new lens, armed with the knowledge to interpret and influence the unspoken dialogue that shapes our relationships.

Let's dive into the captivating realm of non-verbal communication and body language, where actions truly speak louder than words.

3.1: Decoding Gestures and Body Language

In the intricate dance of human communication, gestures and body language form the silent rhythm that often speaks louder than words. This subchapter delves into the fascinating world of non-verbal cues, equipping you with the tools to become a master interpreter of this universal language.

Our bodies are constantly transmitting messages, whether we're aware of it or not. A slight tilt of the head, a crossed arm, or a subtle lean forward can convey volumes about our thoughts, feelings, and intentions. By honing your ability to read these signals, you'll gain invaluable insights into the minds of others, enhancing your social and professional interactions.

But decoding body language isn't just about reading others; it's also about becoming fluent in expressing yourself non-verbally. We'll explore how to harness the power of your own body language to project confidence, warmth, and competence. You'll learn to align your physical presence with your spoken words, creating a harmonious and impactful communication style.

As we embark on this journey, remember that body language is contextual and cultural. A gesture that is seen pleasant in one culture may be offensive in another. We'll navigate these nuances, providing you with a well-rounded understanding of non-verbal communication across different settings and cultures.

By the end of this subchapter, you'll have sharpened your observational skills and developed a keener awareness of your own non-verbal cues. Whether you're in a job interview, on a date, or leading a team meeting, you'll be equipped to read between the lines and communicate more effectively through the silent language of the body.

Let's unlock the secrets hidden in plain sight and master the art of decoding gestures and body language.

3.1.1: How to interpret others' body language

Interpreting body language is like learning to read a new alphabet. Each gesture, posture, and facial expression is a letter, and when combined, they spell out the true message behind the spoken words. Here's how to become fluent in this silent language:

1. Start with the basics: The 3 C's

Context, Clusters, and Congruence are the foundational principles of body language interpretation.

- **Context**: Always consider the situation. A crossed arm in a cold room might simply mean the person is chilly, not defensive.
- **Clusters**: Look for groups of gestures that tell a consistent story. One gesture alone can be misleading.
- **Congruence**: Check if the non-verbal cues match the spoken words. Inconsistency often indicates discomfort or dishonesty.

2. Face facts: Reading facial expressions

The face is typically called the window to the soul, and for good reason. It's a rich source of non-verbal information.

Technique: The Micro-Expression Hunt

Practice observing quick flashes of emotion on people's faces. These micro-expressions often reveal true feelings before they're masked.

3. The eyes have it: Understanding eye contact

Eye contact can indicate interest, honesty, or dominance, depending on its duration and context.

Technique: The 60-70 Rule

In most Western cultures, maintaining eye contact for 60-70% of a conversation is ideal. Too much can seem aggressive, too little evasive.

4. Posture perfect: Decoding body positioning

How a person stands or sits can reveal their comfort level, confidence, and attitude.

Technique: The Posture Scan

Regularly scan people's postures from head to toe. Are they comfortable and open, or are they stiff and closed?

5. Hands-on knowledge: Interpreting hand gestures

Hand movements can emphasize points, express emotions, or betray nervousness.

Technique: The Palm Reader

Open palms frequently indicate honesty and openness, while hidden hands might suggest discomfort or deceit.

Case Study: The Job Interview Revelation

Sarah, a hiring manager, was interviewing candidates for a senior position. One applicant, Tom, had an impressive resume and answered questions articulately. However, Sarah noticed some discrepancies in his body language:

- Tom's smile didn't reach his eyes when discussing his achievements.
- He touched his nose frequently when detailing his past experiences.

- His posture was rigid, with tightly crossed arms.

Using her body language interpretation skills, Sarah probed further. She discovered that Tom had exaggerated some of his accomplishments and wasn't entirely comfortable in high-pressure leadership roles. This insight helped Sarah make a more informed hiring decision, ultimately choosing a candidate whose non-verbal cues aligned with their verbal responses.

3.1.2 : Adjusting your own non-verbal cues for better communication

Now that you can read others' body language, it's time to master your own. By consciously adjusting your non-verbal cues, you can enhance your communication effectiveness and project the image you desire.

1. Strike a power pose

Your posture significantly affects both how others perceive you and how you feel about yourself.

Technique: The Confidence Boost

Before important interactions, stand tall with your feet shoulder-width apart, hands on hips, for two minutes. This "power pose" can increase confidence-boosting hormones.

2. Mirror for rapport

Subtly mimicking the other person's body language can build rapport and make them feel more comfortable.

Technique: The Chameleon Effect

Gradually adopt similar postures, gestures, and speaking pace as your conversation partner. Be subtle to avoid appearing mocking.

3. Open up

Open body language gives the impression that you are more personable and reliable.

Technique: The Openness Inventory

Regularly check your body position. Are your arms crossed? Uncross them. Legs crossed? Plant both feet on the ground. Face someone directly to show engagement.

4. Harness the power of touch

Appropriate touch can build connections, but be mindful of cultural and personal boundaries.

Technique: The Professional Touch

In business settings, a firm handshake is often appropriate. In more casual settings, a light touch on the arm during conversation can build rapport, but always be attuned to the other person's comfort level.

5. Smile with your eyes

A genuine smile involves not just your mouth, but your entire face, particularly your eyes.

Technique: The Duchenne Smile

Practice smiling in a mirror, focusing on engaging your eye muscles. A genuine smile can make you appear both warm and competent.

Case Study: The Presentation Turnaround

Alex, a talented but introverted software engineer, struggled with presenting to large groups. His brilliant ideas were regularly overshadowed by his nervous body language: hunched shoulders, minimal eye contact, and fidgeting hands.

After learning about non-verbal communication, Alex made conscious efforts to adjust his body language:

- He practiced power poses before presentations to boost his confidence.
- During presentations, he made a point to stand tall, make eye contact with audience members, and use open hand gestures to emphasize points.
- He slowed his speaking pace and incorporated deliberate pauses to appear more composed.

The results were transformative. At his next company-wide presentation, Alex's improved body language helped him project confidence and competence. His ideas were received with enthusiasm, and he was soon recognized as a rising star in the company.

Practical Exercise: The Body Language Journal

For one week, keep a "Body Language Journal." Each day, focus on one aspect of non-verbal communication in your interactions:

Day 1: Facial expressions

Day 2: Eye contact

Day 3: Posture

Day 4: Hand gestures

Day 5: Personal space

Day 6: Touch (where appropriate)

Day 7: Overall body language congruence

For each day, record:

1. What specific non-verbal cues did you observe in others?
2. How did you adjust your own non-verbal communication?
3. What effect did these adjustments have on your interactions?

Examine your journal at the conclusion of the week. Reflect on how increased awareness of body language affected your communication. Did you notice any changes in how people responded to you? Did you feel any differently about your interactions?

Remember, mastering body language is an ongoing process. Each interaction is an opportunity to refine your skills in both interpreting and projecting non-verbal cues. As you continue to practice, you'll likely find your communication becoming more effective, your relationships deepening, and your overall social and professional presence enhancing.

By combining keen observation skills with conscious control of your own non-verbal cues, you create a powerful communication style that exudes both warmth and competence. This balanced approach will not only make you a more effective communicator but also a more empathetic and influential presence in both personal and professional settings.

3.2: The Impact of Eye Contact and Space

In the intricate tapestry of non-verbal communication, eye contact and personal space are two of the most powerful threads. These elements can make or break a conversation, build or erode trust, and significantly influence the outcome of our interactions. This subchapter delves into the fascinating world of visual connection and proxemics, exploring how these subtle factors shape our communication experiences.

Eye contact, often referred to as the window to the soul, is a potent tool in our non-verbal arsenal. It can convey a wide range of emotions and intentions, from interest and engagement to dominance or discomfort. Understanding the nuances of eye contact can give you a significant advantage in both personal and professional settings.

Personal space, on the other hand, is the invisible bubble that surrounds each of us. The size of this bubble varies greatly across cultures and contexts, making it a crucial aspect of intercultural communication. By mastering the art of respecting and navigating personal space, you can enhance your ability to connect with others while avoiding unintentional offense.

As we explore these topics, we'll uncover the psychological principles that underpin eye contact and personal space. We'll also examine how these elements contribute to the dual factors of warmth and competence in our interactions. By the end of this subchapter, you'll have a deeper understanding of how to use eye contact effectively and navigate personal space adeptly, enhancing your overall communication skills.

Let's embark on this journey to unravel the mysteries of eye contact and personal space, and discover how these silent yet powerful elements can transform your interactions.

3.2.1 : The psychology behind eye contact

Eye contact is a fundamental aspect of human interaction, deeply rooted in our evolutionary history. It's a powerful tool that can communicate a wealth of information without a single word being spoken. Let's explore the psychological intricacies of this silent conversation:

1. The power of connection

Eye contact stimulates the limbic mirror system in our brains, fostering a sense of emotional connection and empathy.

Technique: The Soul Gaze

Practice maintaining eye contact for 3-5 seconds during conversations. This duration typically feels natural and encourages connection without discomfort.

2. Trust and credibility

Appropriate eye contact can significantly enhance your perceived trustworthiness and credibility.

Technique: The Trustworthy Triangle

When speaking, alternate your gaze between the listener's eyes and the triangular area formed by their eyes and mouth. This creates a sense of engagement without feeling intimidating.

3. Dominance and submission

The duration and intensity of eye contact can convey power dynamics in social interactions.

Technique: The Confidence Balance

In professional settings, aim for equal eye contact when speaking and listening. This projects confidence without appearing domineering.

4. Emotional insight

Our eyes often betray our true feelings, even when our words say otherwise.

Technique: The Emotion Detective

Pay attention to pupil dilation, blink rate, and eye movement. Dilated pupils often indicate interest or excitement, while rapid blinking might suggest stress or discomfort.

5. Cultural considerations

The significance and appropriateness of eye contact can differ greatly between cultures.

Technique: The Cultural Compass

Research eye contact norms before interacting with people from different cultural backgrounds. In some cultures, direct eye contact is respectful, while in others, it may be seen as challenging or disrespectful.

Case Study: The Sales Pitch Transformation

John, a talented but underperforming salesperson, struggled to close deals despite his extensive product knowledge. His manager noticed that John frequently avoided eye contact during crucial moments of his sales pitches, inadvertently undermining his credibility.

After learning about the psychology of eye contact, John made conscious efforts to improve:

- He practiced the Trustworthy Triangle technique during his pitches.
- He maintained eye contact while listening to customers' questions and concerns.
- He used the Soul Gaze technique to build rapport at the beginning of meetings.

The results were remarkable. Within three months, John's sales numbers improved by 40%. Customers reported feeling more connected to him and confident in his product recommendations. John's enhanced eye contact skills had significantly boosted his ability to convey both warmth and competence.

3.2.2 : Understanding personal space across different cultures

Personal space, the invisible bubble that surrounds each of us, is a critical yet often overlooked aspect of non-verbal communication. The size of this bubble and the rules governing it can vary dramatically across cultures, making it a potential minefield in intercultural interactions.

1. The four zones of personal space

Anthropologist Edward T. Hall identified four main distance zones in Western cultures:

- Intimate space (0-18 inches): Reserved for close relationships
- Personal space (18 inches - 4 feet): Comfortable distance for friends
- Social space (4-12 feet): Typical for acquaintances and colleagues
- Public space (12+ feet): Appropriate for public speaking

Technique: The Space Awareness

Practice identifying these zones in your daily interactions. Notice how your comfort level changes as people move between zones.

2. Cultural variations

Personal space norms can differ significantly between cultures.

Technique: The Cultural Space Map

Create a mental map of personal space norms for cultures you frequently interact with. For example, many Middle Eastern cultures are comfortable with closer distances, while some Northern European cultures prefer more space.

3. Context matters

Even within cultures, personal space can vary based on the situation.

Technique: The Context Calibration

Adjust your personal space based on the setting. A crowded subway requires different norms than a formal business meeting.

4. Power and status

Personal space can reflect and reinforce power dynamics.

Technique: The Status Stance

In professional settings, be aware of how you use space. Respect others' personal space to convey respect, but don't be afraid to "own your space" when asserting authority.

5. Touch and personal space

The acceptability of touch varies widely across cultures and contexts.

Technique: The Touch Barometer

Develop sensitivity to others' comfort with touch. Start with less intimate touches (e.g., handshakes) and only progress if clear comfort is shown.

Case Study: The International Business Blunder

Sarah, an American executive, was excited about her company's new partnership with a Brazilian firm. During her first visit to São Paulo, she was taken aback by her Brazilian colleagues' tendency to stand close during conversations and their frequent touches on the arm or shoulder.

Feeling uncomfortable, Sarah consistently backed away and maintained a larger personal space. Her Brazilian counterparts interpreted this as coldness and disinterest, leading to tension in the partnership.

After learning about cultural differences in personal space, Sarah adjusted her approach:

- She researched Brazilian cultural norms, understanding that closer proximity and touch are normal in business settings.
- She practiced staying comfortable with closer distances, reminding herself it was a cultural norm, not an invasion of space.
- She reciprocated light touches when appropriate, building rapport with her Brazilian colleagues.

The result was a dramatic improvement in the partnership. Sarah's Brazilian counterparts noted her increased warmth and engagement, leading to more productive meetings and a stronger business relationship.

Practical Exercise: The Space and Gaze Challenge

For one week, challenge yourself to become more aware of eye contact and personal space in your daily interactions:

Day 1-3: Eye Contact Focus

- Practice the Trustworthy Triangle technique in your conversations.
- Note how different durations of eye contact feel with different people.
- Observe others' eye contact patterns and how they make you feel.

Day 4-7: Personal Space Awareness

- Pay attention to the distance between you and others in various settings.
- Try slightly varying your distance and observe how it affects the interaction.
- If interacting with people from different cultures, research, and practice appropriate personal space norms.

Throughout the week, journal your observations:

1. How did adjusting your eye contact or personal space change the dynamic of your interactions?
2. Did you notice any cultural or contextual differences in how people responded?
3. How did increase awareness of these factors influence your comfort and confidence in communication?

At the end of the week, reflect on your experiences. Consider how you can incorporate your new awareness of eye contact and personal space into your daily communication style.

Remember, mastering the nuances of eye contact and personal space is an ongoing process. These silent yet powerful elements of communication can significantly enhance your ability to connect with others, convey confidence, and navigate diverse cultural settings. By honing these skills, you'll be better equipped to project both warmth and competence in your interactions, leading to more effective and meaningful communication across various personal and professional contexts.

Chapter 4: Storytelling and Persuasion

Once upon a time... Four simple words that have the power to captivate minds, stir emotions, and change perspectives. Welcome to the enchanting world of storytelling and persuasion, where words become wands and narratives transform into spells that can alter reality itself.

In this chapter, we'll unravel the magic behind effective storytelling and its intimate dance partner, persuasion. These twin arts form the bedrock of human communication, transcending cultures and generations to shape our shared experiences and beliefs.

But why are stories so powerful? It's simple: our brains are hardwired for narrative. We don't just enjoy stories; we crave them. They're the vehicle through which we make sense of the world, connect with others, and internalize new ideas. By mastering the art of storytelling, you'll unlock a formidable tool for influence and understanding.

As we explore this fascinating realm, we'll focus on two key factors: emotional resonance and logical coherence. A great story tugs at the heartstrings while satisfying the mind's desire for order and meaning. It's this potent combination that makes storytelling such an effective persuasion technique.

We'll journey through the essential elements of compelling narratives, from character development to plot structure. You'll learn how to craft stories that not only entertain but also persuade, inspire, and motivate. Whether you're a business leader looking to rally your team, a marketer aiming to connect with customers, or simply someone who wants to communicate more effectively, these skills will prove invaluable.

But storytelling is just the beginning. We'll also delve into the art of persuasion, exploring psychological principles and ethical techniques that can help you influence others positively. You'll discover how to build trust, overcome objections, and inspire action through the power of your words.

By the time you finish this chapter, you'll have a toolkit brimming with narrative techniques and persuasive strategies. You'll see the world through the lens of story, recognizing opportunities to connect, convince, and create change wherever you go.

Are you prepared to start this life-changing adventure? Let's turn the page and step into the world where stories shape reality and words wield the power to move mountains.

4.1: Crafting Your Narrative

In the grand tapestry of human communication, storytelling stands out as a vibrant thread that weaves connections, imparts wisdom, and inspires action. Crafting a compelling narrative is an art form that combines creativity with strategy, emotion with logic, and personal experience with universal truths.

This subchapter delves into the heart of narrative creation, exploring the techniques that transform simple anecdotes into powerful tools of persuasion. We'll uncover the secrets behind stories that not only captivate audiences but also drive home key messages and motivate change.

At the core of our exploration are two fundamental factors: emotional resonance and logical coherence. A truly effective narrative must strike a balance between touching the heart and satisfying the mind. It should evoke feelings that resonate deeply with the audience while presenting a clear, logical progression of ideas.

As we journey through this subchapter, we'll examine how to infuse your stories with these crucial elements. You'll learn to create characters that your audience can relate to, craft plots that keep them on the edge of their seats, and deliver messages that linger long after the story ends.

We'll also delve into the structure of impactful stories, exploring frameworks that can amplify your narrative's effectiveness. From the classic hero's journey to modern storytelling techniques, you'll discover how to arrange your narrative elements for maximum impact.

By the end of this subchapter, you'll be equipped with the tools to craft narratives that not only entertain, but also persuade and inspire. Whether you're preparing a business presentation, writing a speech, or simply looking to enhance your everyday communication, these skills will prove invaluable in your quest to become a master storyteller.

Let's embark on this exciting journey of narrative crafting, where words become worlds and stories become catalysts for change.

4.1.1 : How to tell a story that captivates and persuades

Storytelling is an ancient art, but its power remains undiminished in our modern world. A well-told story can bypass our natural defenses, speak directly to our emotions, and leave a lasting impact on our thoughts and actions. Here's how you can harness this power to captivate and persuade:

1. Start with a hook

Begin your story with an intriguing opening that immediately grabs attention. This could be a provocative question, a startling fact, or a vivid scene that plunges the audience into the heart of the action.

Technique: The Curiosity Gap

Make the difference between what your audience already knows and what they would like to know. This cognitive itch will keep them engaged throughout your story.

Example: "Have you ever wondered what would happen if you could read minds? For John Smith, this wasn't just a hypothetical question - it was his new reality."

2. Create relatable characters

Create characters with whom your audience may identify on an emotional level. Even in business contexts, humanizing your narrative makes it more compelling.

Technique: The Empathy Map

Before crafting your character, create an empathy map outlining their thoughts, feelings, actions, and motivations. This will help you create a more three-dimensional, relatable character.

3. Build tension and conflict

Every captivating story needs an element of tension or conflict. This keeps viewers interested in the result.

Technique: The Story Mountain

Plot your narrative along the classic story mountain: exposition, rising action, climax, falling action, and resolution. This structure naturally builds and releases tension.

4. Use vivid, sensory details

Engage your audience's senses to make your story more immersive and memorable.

Technique: The Sensory Palette

For each key scene in your story, list details that appeal to at least three of the five senses.

Example: "The acrid smell of smoke filled her nostrils as she pushed through the creaking door, her fingers tracing the rough, splintered wood."

5. Incorporate emotions

Emotions are the secret sauce that makes stories stick. Use them to create a connection between your audience and your narrative.

Technique: The Emotional Journey

Map out the emotional journey you want your audience to experience. Ensure your story hits these emotional beats.

6. Deliver a clear message

While entertainment is important, persuasive storytelling needs a clear takeaway or call to action.

Technique: The Message Mantra

Distill your core message into a short, memorable phrase. Weave this mantra subtly throughout your story.

Case Study: The Power of Personal Narrative in Marketing

Sarah, a marketing executive for a sustainable clothing brand, was struggling to connect with customers. The company's eco-friendly message wasn't resonating as strongly as she'd hoped. Sarah decided to try a new approach using storytelling.

She crafted a narrative about Maria, a young girl living in a coastal town in the Philippines. The story vividly described how Maria's community was affected by plastic pollution, weaving in sensory details about the once-pristine beaches now littered with plastic waste.

The narrative then shifted to Maria's father, a fisherman who struggled to make ends meet as fish populations declined due to pollution. The story built tension as Maria's family faced increasing hardships.

The turning point came when Maria learned about sustainable practices and started a community initiative to clean the beaches and reduce plastic use. The story concluded with Maria, now a young woman, working as a marine biologist and continuing to fight for ocean conservation.

Throughout the narrative, Sarah subtly wove in information about her company's sustainable practices and how choosing eco-friendly clothing could make a difference. The story's emotional journey - from despair to hope and empowerment - mirrored the message Sarah wanted to convey about the power of individual choices.

The results were remarkable. Engagement on the company's social media platforms skyrocketed, with many customers sharing their own stories about why they chose sustainable products. Sales increased by 30% in the quarter following the campaign launch.

Sarah's success demonstrated the power of a well-crafted narrative in not just captivating an audience, but also in persuading them to take action.

4.1.2 : Structuring stories for maximum impact

The structure of your story is the invisible scaffold that supports your narrative, guiding your audience through an engaging and persuasive journey. A well-structured story can amplify your message, making it more memorable and impactful. Let's explore some powerful structuring techniques:

1. The Classic Three-Act Structure

Your story is broken up into three sections using this tried-and-true format: setup, conflict, and resolve.

Technique: The Story Arc

Map your narrative onto this structure:

- Act 1 (Setup): Present the main conflict, people, and setting.
- Act 2 (Confrontation): Develop the conflict, raise the stakes, and challenge the characters.
- Act 3 (Resolution): Climax and resolution of the conflict, revealing the story's message.

2. The Hero's Journey

This structure, popularized by Joseph Campbell, outlines the typical adventure of a hero.

Technique: The Monomyth Map

Adapt your story to fit key stages of the hero's journey:

- Ordinary World
- Call to Adventure
- Refusal of the Call
- Meeting the Mentor
- Crossing the Threshold
- Tests, Allies, Enemies
- Approach to the Inmost Cave
- Ordeal
- Reward
- The Road Back
- Resurrection
- Return with the Elixir

3. The Mountain Structure

This simple yet effective structure builds tension to a peak before resolving.

Technique: The Elevation Plot

Plot your story along these points:

- Exposition (Base Camp)
- Rising Action (The Climb)
- Climax (The Peak)
- Falling Action (The Descent)
- Resolution (Return to Base)

4. The Nested Loop Structure

This advanced technique involves telling multiple stories or ideas, one inside another.

Technique: The Story Stack

Start with your main story, pause it to tell a related story, then another, before resolving each in reverse order.

Example: A CEO might start telling a story about a company challenge, pause to share an anecdote about a similar personal experience, then a brief story about a historical figure who overcame similar odds, before resolving each story in turn.

5. The Sparkline

This structure contrasts what is with what could be, making it excellent for inspirational or persuasive stories.

Technique: The Reality-Possibility Pendulum

Alternate between describing the current reality and the potential future throughout your narrative.

Case Study: The Sparkline in Action

John, a city council member, wanted to persuade his colleagues to invest in a new public park. Instead of presenting a dry proposal, he structured his presentation as a story using the Sparkline technique.

He began by vividly describing the current state of the neighborhood - a concrete jungle with high crime rates and little community interaction. Then, he painted a picture of what could be - a vibrant green space where families picnic, children play safely, and neighbors connect.

John continued to alternate between these two realities throughout his presentation. He described current health issues in the area, then shared studies about the positive impact of green spaces on physical and mental health. He talked about the current lack of community events, then described potential festivals and gatherings in the new park.

By the end of his presentation, John had taken his audience on an emotional journey. They had experienced the stark contrast between the current reality and the potential future, making the need for change feel urgent and compelling.

The result? The council voted unanimously to approve the park project. John's use of the Sparkline structure had transformed a standard proposal into a powerful, persuasive narrative.

Practical Exercise: The Story Structure Challenge

Over the next week, challenge yourself to experiment with different story structures:

Day 1-2: The Classic Three-Act Structure

- Choose a personal anecdote or a business case study.
- Map it onto the three-act structure.
- Practice telling this structured version to a friend or colleague.

Day 3-4: The Hero's Journey

- Take the same story and adapt it to fit the stages of the Hero's Journey.
- Notice how this changes the emotional impact of your story.

Day 5-6: The Sparkline

- Choose a topic you're passionate about changing.
- Create a Sparkline structure, alternating between current reality and potential future.
- Practice delivering this as a short, persuasive speech.

Day 7: Reflection and Integration

- Reflect on which structure felt most natural to you.
- Consider which structure might be most effective for different types of stories or audiences.
- Choose one structure to focus on mastering in the coming weeks.

Remember, the key to impactful storytelling lies in the seamless integration of structure with content. As you practice these techniques, focus on maintaining the emotional resonance and logical coherence that form the backbone of persuasive narratives.

By mastering these structuring techniques, you'll be able to craft stories that not only captivate your audience but also guide them towards the conclusions and actions you desire. Whether you're pitching a business idea, delivering a keynote speech, or simply sharing an anecdote with friends, these skills will elevate your storytelling to new heights of effectiveness and impact.

4.2: The Power of Stories in Business and Life

Stories are the universal language of human experience. They transcend cultural barriers, bridge generational gaps, and have the unique ability to transform complex ideas into relatable, memorable narratives. In the realms of business and personal life, storytelling emerges as a formidable tool for communication, influence, and inspiration.

This subchapter explores the profound impact of storytelling in both professional and personal contexts. We'll delve into why stories are not just entertaining, but essential for effective influence and persuasion. Through real-life examples and case studies, we'll illustrate how successful individuals and organizations have harnessed the power of narrative to achieve remarkable outcomes.

At the heart of our exploration are two fundamental factors: emotional connection and cognitive resonance. A well-crafted story has the power to touch hearts and stimulate minds simultaneously, creating a lasting impression that facts and figures alone cannot match.

As we journey through this subchapter, you'll discover how stories can be used to:

- Build brand loyalty and customer engagement
- Motivate teams and inspire innovation
- Communicate complex ideas in accessible ways
- Create personal connections and foster empathy
- Drive change and inspire action

We'll examine the psychological principles behind storytelling's effectiveness and provide practical strategies for incorporating storytelling into your professional and personal communication.

By the end of this subchapter, you'll have a deeper understanding of why stories matter in all aspects of life, and how you can leverage this powerful tool to enhance your influence, build stronger relationships, and achieve your goals.

Let's embark on this exploration of the transformative power of stories, and uncover how you can harness this ancient art to create modern-day impact.

4.2.1: Why storytelling is essential for influence?

In a world inundated with information, the ability to influence others has become a crucial skill. Whether you're a business leader, a marketer, a teacher, or simply someone trying to make a difference in your community, storytelling emerges as an indispensable tool for exerting influence. Here's why:

1. Stories create emotional connections

Human beings are inherently emotional creatures. While logic and facts have their place, it's emotions that often drive decision-making and behavior.

Technique: The Emotional Anchor

Identify the core emotion you want your audience to feel, and build your story around evoking that emotion.

Example: A non-profit organization fighting hunger doesn't just present statistics. Instead, they tell the story of Sarah, a single mother struggling to feed her children, creating an emotional connection that motivates donors to act.

2. Stories make complex ideas accessible

In an era of information overload, stories provide a framework for understanding and remembering complex concepts.

Technique: The Analogy Approach

Use analogies or metaphors to explain complex ideas through familiar concepts.

Example: When explaining how a company's different departments work together, a CEO might use the analogy of a sports team, with each department playing a crucial role in scoring the "goal" of company success.

3. Stories are more memorable than facts

Our brains are wired to remember stories better than isolated facts or figures.

Technique: The Narrative Wrapper

Wrap important data or information within a story to make it more memorable.

Example: Instead of simply stating that customer satisfaction increased by 25%, a company might tell the story of how they identified a problem through a customer's feedback and the journey they took to improve their service.

4. Stories build trust and credibility

Sharing personal stories or case studies can establish authenticity and build trust with your audience.

Technique: The Vulnerability Vignette

Share a story that demonstrates your own challenges or failures, and how you overcame them.

Example: A leadership coach might share a story about a time when they struggled with public speaking, and how they overcame this challenge, to connect with clients facing similar issues.

5. Stories inspire action

A well-told story can motivate people to take action in ways that simple requests or commands cannot.

Technique: The Hero's Call

Structure your story so that the audience sees themselves as the hero who can make a difference.

Example: An environmental organization might tell the story of how small actions by individuals led to significant positive changes in a local ecosystem, inspiring others to take similar actions.

Case Study: The Power of Storytelling in Crisis Management

When a major tech company faced a severe data breach, their initial response was a textbook example of what not to do. They issued a dry, jargon-filled statement that left customers feeling confused and angry.

Recognizing their mistake, the company's new CEO decided to take a different approach. She crafted a narrative that acknowledged the company's failure, explained the situation in simple terms, and outlined their plan moving forward.

The CEO began with a personal story of how she, too, had once been a victim of identity theft. She described the fear and frustration she felt, immediately connecting with the emotions of affected customers. This vulnerability helped to rebuild trust.

Next, she used an analogy to explain the data breach, comparing it to a thief finding a hidden key to a house. This made the complex technical issue understandable to all customers.

She then shared stories of the company's employees working round the clock to fix the issue, humanizing the company and demonstrating their commitment.

Finally, she outlined the steps they were taking to prevent future breaches, weaving in a vision of a safer digital future that customers could be part of by staying with the company.

The result was transformative. Instead of a mass exodus of customers, many expressed appreciation for the honest, clear communication. The company's stock, which had plummeted after the breach, began to recover. The story-based approach had turned a potential disaster into an opportunity to strengthen customer relationships.

4.2.2: Real-life examples of successful storytelling

Storytelling's power isn't just theoretical; it's proven time and again in real-world scenarios. Let's explore some compelling examples of how individuals and organizations have used storytelling to achieve remarkable results:

1. Apple's "Think Different" Campaign

When Steve Jobs returned to Apple in 1997, the company was struggling. Instead of focusing on product features, Jobs launched the "Think Different" campaign, telling a story about creativity and innovation.

The campaign featured images of iconic "crazy ones" who changed the world, from Einstein to Gandhi. The narrative positioned Apple not just as a computer company, but as a brand for creative, innovative individuals who want to make a difference.

This storytelling approach didn't just sell products; it created a devoted community of Apple users who saw themselves as part of this narrative of creativity and innovation.

2. Charity: Water's Founder Story

Scott Harrison, founder of Charity: Water, uses his personal story to drive donations and engagement. Harrison tells of his transformation from a New York City club promoter to a volunteer on a hospital ship in Liberia, where he witnessed the impact of unclean water firsthand.

This personal narrative creates an emotional connection with potential donors, making the issue of clean water access more tangible and urgent. By sharing his journey, Harrison inspires others to be part of the solution.

3. Airbnb's User Stories

Airbnb has masterfully used storytelling to build trust in their platform. Instead of focusing solely on the features of their service, they share stories of hosts and guests from around the world.

These stories humanize the Airbnb experience, showcasing the cultural exchanges and personal connections that can happen through home-sharing. This narrative approach has helped Airbnb overcome initial skepticism about staying in strangers' homes and build a global community.

4. Dove's Real Beauty Campaign

Dove revolutionized beauty advertising with its "Real Beauty" campaign. Instead of using traditional models, Dove told the stories of real women, challenging conventional beauty standards.

This storytelling approach not only boosted sales but also created a movement, inspiring women to embrace their natural beauty. The campaign demonstrated how storytelling can be used to challenge societal norms and create positive change.

5. Microsoft's "Stories" Initiative

Microsoft launched a storytelling initiative to change public perception of the company as purely a software giant. They began sharing stories of how their technology is used in various fields, from healthcare to education.

One powerful story was that of a young girl with dyslexia who used Microsoft's learning tools to improve her reading skills. By focusing on the human impact of their technology, Microsoft has been able to connect emotionally with their audience and showcase their broader impact on society.

Case Study: The Significant Objects Project

The Significant Objects project, started by Rob Walker and Joshua Glenn, provides a fascinating look at the pure power of storytelling. The experiment was simple: they purchased cheap trinkets from thrift stores and yard sales, then asked writers to create fictional stories about these objects.

The objects, along with their new stories, were then listed on eBay. The results were astounding. Items that had been purchased for an average of $1.25 sold for nearly $8,000 in total. For example, a horse-head bottle opener bought for $0.99 sold for $62.95 after being paired with a short story.

This experiment demonstrates the remarkable ability of stories to add perceived value. The physical objects hadn't changed, but the addition of a narrative completely transformed how people viewed them.

Practical Exercise: Your Story of Influence

Over the next week, practice using storytelling to influence in your personal or professional life:

Day 1-2: Identify Your Story

- Think of a time when you overcame a challenge or learned an important lesson.
- Write down the key elements: the setting, the conflict, the turning point, and the resolution.

Day 3-4: Craft Your Narrative

- Using the storytelling techniques we've discussed, shape your experience into a compelling narrative.
- Focus on creating emotional resonance and ensuring your story has a clear message or takeaway.

Day 5-6: Practice and Refine

- Try sharing your tale with a friend or relative.
- Ask for feedback: Did the story resonate? Was the message clear? What could be improved?

Day 7: Real-World Application

- Find an opportunity to use your story in a real-life situation, whether it's in a work presentation, a social gathering, or a one-on-one conversation.
- Reflect on the impact: How did people respond? Did you notice any changes in their perceptions or actions?

Remember, the goal isn't just to tell a good story, but to influence and inspire. As you practice, focus on how your story can create an emotional connection while also delivering a meaningful message.

By integrating storytelling into your communication toolkit, you'll enhance your ability to influence, inspire, and connect with others in all areas of life. Whether you're leading a team, building a brand, or simply trying to make a difference in your community, the power of story will be your ally in achieving your goals.

Chapter 5: Navigating Challenging Communication Scenarios

Life rarely follows a script, and neither does communication. We often find ourselves in situations where the stakes are high, emotions run deep, and the path forward seems unclear. These are the moments that test our communication skills to their limits, pushing us to grow and adapt in ways we never thought possible.

In this chapter, we'll dive headfirst into the turbulent waters of challenging communication scenarios. From delivering tough news to managing conflict,

from negotiating high-stakes deals to addressing sensitive topics, we'll explore the strategies and techniques that can turn potential communication disasters into opportunities for understanding and growth.

At the core of our exploration are two fundamental factors: emotional intelligence and adaptive communication. These twin pillars will serve as our compass as we navigate through treacherous conversational terrain.

Emotional intelligence allows us to recognize and manage our own emotions while empathizing with others. It's the foundation that keeps us steady when tensions rise and misunderstandings threaten to derail conversations.

Adaptive communication, on the other hand, is our ability to flex our communication style to meet the unique demands of each situation. It's about reading the room, adjusting our approach on the fly, and finding creative ways to bridge gaps in understanding.

As we continue in this chapter, you will learn:

- How to deliver difficult messages with clarity and compassion
- Techniques for de-escalating heated conversations

- Techniques for overcoming communication barriers caused by cultural differences
- Strategies for constructively addressing and resolving disputes
- Methods for communicating effectively under pressure

Each section will be packed with real-world examples, practical exercises, and actionable advice. By the time you reach the end of this chapter, you'll be equipped with a versatile toolkit of communication strategies, ready to face even the most daunting conversational challenges with confidence and skill.

So, brace yourself for a journey into the heart of communication complexity. The road ahead may be challenging, but the rewards - stronger relationships, better outcomes, and personal growth - are well worth the effort. Let's embark on this exploration of communication mastery together, and unlock the power to navigate any conversation with grace and effectiveness.

5.1: Strategies for Difficult Conversations

Whether in regular contacts, professional situations, or personal connections, difficult talks are an inescapable part of life. These conversations often involve sensitive topics, conflicting viewpoints, or high-stakes outcomes, making them challenging to navigate. However, mastering the art of handling these conversations can lead to improved relationships, better problem-solving, and personal growth.

In this subchapter, we'll explore effective strategies for managing difficult conversations with grace and skill. Our focus will be on two critical aspects: maintaining composure in tense situations and resolving conflicts without compromising your position.

The two main factors we'll consider throughout this discussion are emotional regulation and assertive communication. Emotional regulation involves managing your own feelings and reactions, while assertive communication allows you to express your thoughts and needs clearly and respectfully.

Acquiring these skills will increase your ability to:

- Remain composed under pressure
- Express your views effectively without escalating conflicts
- Actively listen and understand the viewpoints of others
- Look for areas of agreement and strive toward win-win solutions

We'll examine real-life scenarios, share practical techniques, and provide actionable advice to help you transform difficult conversations from sources of stress into opportunities for understanding and growth.

As we delve into this topic, remember that mastering difficult conversations is a journey, not a destination. Each challenging interaction is a chance to refine your skills and deepen your understanding of human communication.

Let's begin our exploration of these vital communication strategies, starting with techniques to maintain calm and control in high-pressure situations.

5.1.1: How to keep calm and maintain control in tense situations?

Remaining calm during tense conversations is often easier said than done. However, it's a crucial skill that can dramatically improve the outcomes of difficult interactions. Let's explore some effective strategies for maintaining composure when the pressure is on.

1. Practice mindful breathing

One of the simplest yet most powerful techniques for staying calm is controlled breathing. When we're stressed, our breathing frequently becomes shallow and rapid, exacerbating feelings of anxiety.

Technique: The 4-7-8 Breath

- Take a four-second, quiet breath through your nose
- Hold your breath for 7 seconds
- For eight seconds, exhale fully through your mouth
- Repeat this cycle 3-4 times

This technique helps activate your body's relaxation response, reducing stress and promoting clarity of thought.

2. Use the STOP method

When you feel yourself becoming overwhelmed, the STOP method can help you regain control:

S - Stop what you're doing

T - Take a breath

O - Observe your thoughts and feelings

P - Proceed with a more mindful response

This brief pause can prevent knee-jerk reactions and allow for more thoughtful responses.

3. Employ cognitive reframing

How we perceive a situation greatly affects our emotional response. By reframing negative thoughts, we can reduce stress and maintain control.

For instance, try rephrasing the conversation as "This is an opportunity to improve understanding and find a solution," rather than "This conversation is going to be a disaster."

4. Utilize physical grounding techniques

When emotions run high, connecting with your physical surroundings can help you stay grounded.

Technique: The 5-4-3-2-1 Method

Identify:

5 things you can see

4 things you can touch

3 things you can hear

2 things you can smell

1 thing you can taste

This exercise shifts your focus away from stressful thoughts and back to the present moment.

5. Prepare and visualize success

Anticipating potential challenges and visualizing positive outcomes can boost confidence and reduce anxiety.

Technique: Scenario Planning

Before a difficult conversation, spend some time:

- Identifying potential challenges or objections
- Preparing thoughtful responses
- Visualizing yourself responding calmly and effectively

Case Study: The Calm Manager

Sarah, a project manager, was known for her ability to stay cool under pressure. During a high-stakes client meeting, tensions rose when the client expressed dissatisfaction with recent project delays.

Instead of becoming defensive, Sarah took a deep breath and employed the STOP method. She paused, acknowledged the client's concerns, and reframed the situation in her mind as an opportunity to strengthen the relationship.

Sarah then calmly explained the reasons for the delays and proposed a detailed plan to get back on track. Her composed demeanor helped de-escalate the situation, and the client left the meeting feeling heard and confident in the team's ability to deliver.

5.1.2 : Defusing arguments without sacrificing your point

Disagreements are a natural part of human interaction, but they don't have to escalate into full-blown arguments. The key is to express your views assertively while still showing respect for the other person's perspective. Here are strategies to help you defuse tensions without compromising your position.

1. Use "I" statements

"I" statements allow you to express your thoughts and feelings without sounding accusatory, reducing the likelihood of putting others on the defensive.

Instead of: "You always interrupt me!"

Try: "I feel frustrated when I'm not able to finish my thoughts."

2. Practice active listening

Genuinely listening to the other person can go a long way in defusing tension. It shows respect and often leads to the other person being more receptive to your views.

Technique: Reflective Listening

- Pay full attention to the speaker
- Paraphrase what you've heard to ensure understanding
- Ask clarifying questions

Example: "If I understand correctly, you're saying that..."

3. Seek common ground

Finding areas of agreement, no matter how small, can create a foundation for resolving larger disagreements.

Technique: The Agreement Framework

- Start by acknowledging points you agree on
- Employ expressions such as "We agree that..." or "We both want..."
- Build on these shared interests to address areas of disagreement

4. Use the "Yes, and..." approach

This technique, borrowed from improvisational theater, allows you to acknowledge the other person's point while still adding your own perspective.

Instead of: "No, but..."

Try: "Yes, and additionally..."

5. Focus on interests, not positions

Frequently, conflicts arise from differing positions, but underlying interests may be compatible.

Technique: The Interest Exploration

- Ask "Why is this important to you?"
- Explain why the matter is important to you.
- Look for ways to satisfy both parties' underlying interests

Case Study: The Team Leader's Dilemma

Alex, a team leader, faced a challenge when two team members, Jess and Mark, strongly disagreed on the approach to a critical project. The disagreement was becoming heated and threatening team morale.

Alex decided to intervene using the strategies we've discussed:

- He started by using "I" statements to express his concerns about the impact of the conflict on the team.
- He then practiced active listening, giving both Jess and Mark a chance to explain their positions without interruption. He used reflective listening to ensure he understood each perspective correctly.
- Alex then focused on finding common ground, pointing out that both Jess and Mark were passionate about the project's success.
- He employed the "Yes, and..." approach to acknowledge the merits of both ideas while suggesting a potential compromise.
- Finally, Alex guided the conversation towards exploring the underlying interests behind each position. It turned out that Jess was concerned about meeting the deadline, while Mark was focused on ensuring quality.

By understanding these underlying interests, the team was able to craft a solution that addressed both concerns. The conflict was defused, and the team emerged stronger, with a more robust plan for the project.

Practical Exercise: The Disagreement Diary

Over the next week, keep a "Disagreement Diary" to practice and reflect on your conflict resolution skills:

Day 1-2: Awareness

- Notice when you encounter disagreements or potential conflicts
- Write down the situation, the emotions you felt, and your initial reaction

Day 3-4: Strategy Selection

- For each situation, identify which of the strategies discussed in this chapter might have been helpful
- Write down how you could have applied these strategies

Day 5-6: Implementation

- In new disagreements, consciously try to apply the strategies you've learned
- Note what worked well and what was challenging

Day 7: Reflection

- Review your diary entries
- Reflect on your progress and areas for improvement
- Set specific goals for continued growth in handling disagreements

Remember, the goal isn't to win every argument, but to communicate effectively and maintain positive relationships even in the face of disagreement. With practice, you'll find yourself better equipped to navigate conflicts constructively, turning potential arguments into opportunities for mutual understanding and collaborative problem-solving.

By mastering these strategies for difficult conversations, you'll not only improve your personal and professional relationships but also develop greater resilience and emotional intelligence. These skills will serve you well in all aspects of life, helping you to navigate even the most challenging communication scenarios with confidence and grace.

5.2: Overcoming Communication Anxiety

Communication anxiety is a common challenge that affects many people, often hindering personal and professional growth. Whether it's the fear of public speaking or the nervousness that comes with social interactions, anxiety can significantly impact our ability to express ourselves effectively and connect with others.

In this subchapter, we'll explore practical strategies to overcome communication anxiety and build confidence in various social settings. Our focus will be on two critical areas: managing social and public speaking anxiety, and developing self-assurance in everyday conversations.

The two main factors we'll consider throughout this discussion are cognitive restructuring and exposure therapy. Cognitive restructuring involves identifying and challenging negative thought patterns, while exposure therapy gradually increases comfort with anxiety-inducing situations.

By developing skills in these areas, you'll be better equipped to:

- Manage nervousness in social and public speaking situations
- Reframe anxious thoughts into more balanced perspectives
- Build resilience through gradual exposure to challenging scenarios
- Cultivate authentic confidence in various communication contexts

We'll examine real-life examples, share evidence-based techniques, and provide actionable advice to help you transform anxiety into confidence. Remember, overcoming communication anxiety is a journey of self-discovery and growth. Each step forward, no matter how small, is a victory worth celebrating.

As we delve into this topic, keep in mind that everyone's experience with anxiety is unique. The strategies we'll discuss can be adapted to suit your individual needs and circumstances. Let's begin our exploration of these empowering communication strategies, starting with techniques to manage social and public speaking anxiety.

5.2.1 : Techniques to manage social and public speaking anxiety

Social and public speaking anxiety can be paralyzing, but with the right tools and mindset, it's possible to transform this fear into fuel for effective communication. Let's explore some proven techniques to help you manage these common forms of anxiety.

1. Practice controlled breathing

Anxiety often manifests physically through rapid, shallow breathing. Controlling your breath can help calm your nervous system and reduce anxiety symptoms.

Technique: Box Breathing

- Inhale slowly for 4 counts
- Hold your breath for 4 counts
- Exhale slowly for 4 counts
- Hold your breath for 4 counts
- Repeat for 2-3 minutes

This technique can be discreetly used before or during anxiety-inducing situations to promote calmness.

2. Challenge negative thoughts

Anxiety often stems from negative self-talk and catastrophic thinking. By challenging these thoughts, you can reduce their impact on your confidence.

Technique: The ABCDE Method

A - Activating Event: Identify the situation causing anxiety

B - Beliefs: Recognize the negative thoughts or beliefs about the situation

C - Consequences: Notice how these beliefs affect your emotions and behavior

D - Dispute: Challenge these beliefs with evidence and alternative perspectives

E - Effect: Observe how your emotions and behavior change with this new perspective

Example:

A - Giving a presentation at work

B - "I'll erase all my memories and embarrass myself "

C - Increased anxiety, considering backing out

D - "I've gotten ready thoroughly and have delivered successful presentations in the past "

E - Feeling more confident and ready to face the challenge

3. Utilize visualization techniques

Positive visualization can help reduce anxiety by familiarizing your mind with successful outcomes.

Technique: Mental Rehearsal

- Locate a peaceful area and shut your eyes
- Vividly imagine yourself successfully navigating the anxiety-inducing situation
- Engage all your senses in this visualization
- Practice this regularly, especially before challenging events

4. Implement gradual exposure

Over time, resilience can be developed by exposing oneself to anxiety-inducing events progressively.

Technique: Anxiety Ladder

- Create a list of anxiety-inducing situations, ranked from least to most challenging
- Start with the scenario that causes the least amount of worry and work your way up.
- Honor every accomplishment, no matter how minor.

Example Anxiety Ladder for Public Speaking:

1. Speaking up in a small group of friends
2. Asking a question in a large meeting
3. Giving a short presentation to a small team
4. Presenting to a larger department
5. Speaking at a company-wide event

5. Focus on your message, not yourself

Shifting focus from self-consciousness to the content of your message can significantly reduce anxiety.

Technique: The Message-Centered Approach

- Remember the significance of your message
- Focus on how your information can benefit your audience
- Visualize yourself as a conduit for valuable information

Case Study: The Anxious Presenter

Emma, a talented marketing specialist, struggled with severe public speaking anxiety. Whenever she had to present her ideas to clients or colleagues, she would experience intense nervousness, sometimes even considering changing careers to avoid these situations.

Determined to overcome her fear, Emma decided to implement the techniques we've discussed:

1. She practiced box breathing before presentations to calm her nerves.
2. Using the ABCDE method, Emma challenged her negative thoughts about public speaking, reminding herself of past successes and her thorough preparation.
3. She regularly visualized herself giving confident, impactful presentations.
4. Emma created an anxiety ladder and gradually exposed herself to more challenging speaking situations, starting with small team meetings and working her way up to client presentations.
5. During presentations, she focused on the value of her message to the audience rather than her own nervousness.

Emma saw her anxiety significantly decrease over time. While she still felt some nervousness before big presentations, it no longer overwhelmed her. Instead, she learned to channel that energy into delivering engaging and persuasive presentations.

5.2.2: Building confidence in conversations

Confidence in everyday conversations is crucial for building relationships, advancing professionally, and enjoying social interactions. Let's explore strategies to help you cultivate genuine confidence in various communication contexts.

1. Prepare conversation starters

Having a few conversation starters ready can boost confidence and ease anxiety in social situations.

Technique: The FORM Method

Prepare questions related to:

F - Family

O - Occupation

R - Recreation

M - Motivation

Example questions:

- "What's your family's favorite weekend activity?"
- "What do you enjoy most about your work?"
- "Have you taken up any new hobbies recently?"
- "What inspired you to enter your field?"

2. Practice active listening

Focusing on listening can reduce self-consciousness and lead to more engaging conversations.

Technique: The HEAR Method

H - Halt: Stop talking and focus on the speaker

E - Engage: Show you're listening through nonverbal cues

A - Anticipate: Consider the next words the speaker might say

R - Respond: Offer thoughtful responses or follow-up questions

3. Embrace authenticity

Being genuine in your interactions can reduce anxiety and build real connections.

Technique: The Authenticity Check

Before speaking, ask yourself:

- Is this true to who I am?
- Does this reflect my genuine thoughts or feelings?
- Am I saying this to impress, or to express?

4. Use power posing

Your body language can influence your mental state and perceived confidence.

Technique: The Two-Minute Power Pose

- Before entering a social situation, find a private space
- Stand tall with your feet apart and hands on your hips
- Hold this pose for two minutes
- Notice how your confidence level changes

5. Reframe mistakes as learning opportunities

Embracing a growth mindset can help build resilience and reduce fear of social missteps.

Technique: The Learning Log

- Following social encounters, consider what worked and what could be done better
- For any perceived mistakes, ask:
- What can I learn from this?
- How can I use this experience to improve future interactions?

Case Study: The Networking Novice

Alex, a recent graduate, struggled with confidence in networking events. He would often stand in corners, avoiding interaction due to fear of saying the wrong thing or being judged.

Determined to improve, Alex implemented the strategies we've discussed:

1. He prepared conversation starters using the FORM method, giving him a sense of readiness.
2. Alex focused on active listening, which took the pressure off always having to speak and led to more engaging conversations.
3. He practiced authenticity, sharing his genuine interests and opinions instead of trying to impress others.
4. Before events, Alex would do a two-minute power pose in a restroom stall, which helped boost his confidence.
5. After each event, he would reflect on his interactions, viewing any awkward moments as opportunities for growth rather than failures.

Over time, Alex noticed a significant improvement in his networking skills and overall social confidence. He began to enjoy these events, making valuable connections and even looking forward to future networking opportunities.

Practical Exercise: The Confidence Building Challenge

Over the next week, challenge yourself to build confidence in your daily interactions:

Day 1-2: Conversation Starters

- Prepare three conversation starters using the FORM method
- Use at least one in a conversation each day

Day 3-4: Active Listening

- Practice the HEAR method in your daily interactions
- Reflect on how this impacts your conversations

Day 5-6: Authenticity Check

- Before speaking in social situations, do a quick authenticity check
- Note how this affects your comfort level and the quality of your interactions

Day 7: Reflection and Goal Setting

- Review your experiences from the week
- Identify areas of improvement and success
- Set specific goals for continuing to build your conversation confidence

Remember, building confidence is a gradual process. Celebrate your progress, no matter how small, and be patient with yourself as you grow. With consistent practice and a positive mindset, you'll find yourself becoming more confident and at ease in various communication scenarios.

By mastering these techniques for managing anxiety and building confidence, you'll not only improve your communication skills but also enhance your overall quality of life. These strategies will empower you to express yourself authentically, build meaningful connections, and seize opportunities that you might have previously avoided due to anxiety.

Chapter 6: Digital and Cross-Cultural Communication

In today's interconnected world, the ability to communicate effectively across digital platforms and diverse cultures has become an essential skill. As our global village continues to shrink, thanks to technological advancements, we find ourselves interacting with people from various backgrounds and navigating an ever-expanding digital landscape.

This chapter delves into the intricate world of digital and cross-cultural communication, exploring the challenges and opportunities that arise when we extend our conversations beyond traditional boundaries. We'll examine how the digital realm has transformed the way we connect, share ideas, and build relationships, while also considering the nuances of communicating across cultural divides.

Two primary factors will guide our exploration: digital literacy and cultural intelligence. Digital literacy encompasses the skills needed to navigate, evaluate, and create content in the digital world. Cultural intelligence, on the other hand, refers to the ability to understand, appreciate, and effectively interact with people from different cultural backgrounds.

As we journey through this chapter, we'll uncover strategies to:

- Leverage digital tools to enhance communication effectiveness
- Avoid common challenges in online interactions
- Develop cultural sensitivity and adaptability in global communications
- Bridge language barriers and interpret non-verbal cues across cultures

Whether you're a business professional collaborating with international teams, a student participating in online forums, or simply someone looking to broaden your horizons. This chapter will equip you with the knowledge and skills to thrive in our digitally connected, culturally diverse world.

Prepare to embark on a fascinating exploration of how technology and culture intersect in the realm of communication. By the end of this chapter, you'll be better prepared to engage confidently and respectfully in our global digital society.

6.1: Mastering Digital Communication

In the digital age, our ability to communicate effectively through various online platforms has become crucial. From crafting professional emails to navigating social media, and from participating in virtual meetings to building online networks, digital communication skills are essential for personal and professional success.

This subchapter focuses on two key aspects of digital communication: email etiquette and social media best practices, and building rapport in virtual meetings and online networking. We'll explore strategies to enhance your digital communication skills, ensuring your messages are clear, professional, and impactful across various online platforms.

The two main factors we'll consider throughout this discussion are digital literacy and online etiquette. Digital literacy involves understanding and using digital tools effectively, while online etiquette encompasses the norms and expectations of respectful behavior in digital spaces.

By building expertise in these areas, you'll be better positioned to:

- Craft clear and professional emails
- Navigate social media platforms effectively
- Build meaningful connections in virtual meetings
- Expand your professional network online

We'll examine real-world examples, share practical tips, and provide actionable advice to help you become a more effective digital communicator. Remember, mastering digital communication is an ongoing process that requires practice and adaptation to evolving technologies and norms.

As we delve into this topic, keep in mind that effective digital communication often mirrors the principles of good face-to-face communication, with some unique considerations for the online environment. Let's begin our exploration of these essential digital communication skills, starting with email etiquette and social media best practices.

6.1.1 : Email etiquette and social media best practices

In our increasingly digital world, email and social media have become primary channels for both personal and professional communication. Mastering the etiquette and best practices for these platforms is crucial for effective communication and maintaining a positive online presence.

Email Etiquette

1. Craft clear and concise subject lines

Your subject line is the first thing recipients see. Make it informative and specific to increase the chances of your email being read promptly.

Best Practice: Use action-oriented subject lines

Instead of: "Meeting"

Try : "Action Needed: Team Budget Meeting – Reply by Friday"

2. Start with a proper greeting

Begin your email with an appropriate salutation based on your relationship with the recipient and the context of your communication.

Examples:

- Formal: "Dear Dr. Smith,"
- Semi-formal: "Hello Ms. Johnson,"
- Casual: "Hi Sam,"

3. Keep your message clear and concise

Respect your recipient's time by getting to the point quickly and organizing your thoughts logically.

Technique: The BLUF (Bottom Line Up Front) method

- Start with your main point or request
- Follow with supporting details or explanations

Example:

"I'm reaching out to request your approval for the new marketing budget. The proposed amount is $50,000, reflecting a 10% increase from last year. This additional funding will enable us to enhance our digital advertising initiatives. A detailed breakdown is attached for your review."

4. Use professional language and tone

Maintain a professional tone, even in less formal emails. Avoid slang, excessive punctuation, or all caps.

5. Proofread before sending

Always review your email for typos, grammatical errors, and clarity before hitting send.

Technique: The Three-Pass Review

1. Check for overall clarity and structure
2. Review for grammar and spelling
3. Double-check all names, dates, and important details

Social Media Best Practices

1. Choose the right platform for your message

Different social media platforms cater to distinct audiences and follow unique norms. Choose the most appropriate platform for your content and audience.

Example:

- LinkedIn for professional networking and industry insights
- Instagram for visual content and brand storytelling
- Twitter for news, quick updates, and real-time engagement

2. Maintain a consistent brand voice

Whether posting for personal or professional reasons, maintain a consistent tone that aligns with your personal or brand identity.

3. Engage authentically with your audience

Reply to comments, messages, and mentions promptly and sincerely.

Technique: The 3R's of Social Media Engagement

- Respond: Answer questions and acknowledge comments
- Repost: Share relevant content from your followers or industry
- Reach out: Proactively engage with others' content

4. Be mindful of privacy and security

Always consider the potential long-term implications of your posts and adjust your privacy settings accordingly.

5. Use hashtags strategically

Hashtags can increase the visibility of your posts, but use them judiciously and relevantly.

Best Practice: Research popular and relevant hashtags in your industry or niche, and use a mix of broad and specific tags.

Case Study: The Social Media Turnaround

Sarah, a small business owner, struggled to gain traction on social media. Her posts were inconsistent, lacked engagement, and didn't reflect her brand's personality. After implementing the best practices we've discussed, Sarah saw a significant improvement in her social media presence:

1. She chose to focus on Instagram and Facebook, where her target audience was most active.
2. Sarah developed a consistent brand voice that was friendly, informative, and aligned with her business values.
3. She began responding promptly to all comments and messages, building a loyal community.
4. Sarah started using relevant hashtags, increasing her posts' visibility.
5. She shared a mix of product photos, behind-the-scenes content, and customer testimonials, providing value to her followers.

Within three months, Sarah's follower count had doubled, and engagement on her posts increased by 150%. More importantly, she started seeing a direct impact on her business, with customers mentioning her social media content when making purchases.

As remote work and digital networking become increasingly common, the ability to build meaningful connections in virtual environments is crucial. Let's explore strategies to enhance your presence in virtual meetings and expand your professional network online.

Virtual Meeting Rapport

1. Prepare your virtual environment

Ensure your background, lighting, and audio are professional and distraction-free.

Technique: The Virtual Meeting Checklist

- Check your technology (camera, microphone, internet connection)
- Select a quiet spot with adequate lighting
- Use a neutral or professional background
- Position your camera at eye level

2. Practice active listening and engagement

Show that you're present and engaged throughout the meeting.

Best Practices:

- Keep eye contact by looking at the camera
- Employ nonverbal cues such as nodding and smiling.
- Take notes to stay focused and show interest
- Minimize multitasking

3. Use visual aids effectively

When presenting, use clear and concise visual aids to enhance understanding and engagement.

Technique: The 5x5 Rule

- Limit to 5 bullet points per slide
- Use no more than 5 words per bullet point

4. Encourage participation

Create an inclusive environment where all participants feel at ease contributing.

Strategies:

- Use polls or breakout rooms for larger meetings
- Call on individuals by name for input
- Promote the use of chat features for questions and comments.

5. Follow up after the meeting

Solidify connections made during the meeting with prompt follow-up.

Best Practice: Send a personalized message within 24 hours, referencing specific points discussed in the meeting.

Online Networking

1. Optimize your online profiles

Ensure your professional online profiles accurately reflect your skills, experience, and goals.

Technique: The 3C's of Profile Optimization

- Clear: Use concise, jargon-free language
- Complete: Fill out all relevant sections
- Consistent: Maintain a consistent personal brand across platforms

2. Engage regularly with your network

Stay active on professional networking platforms by sharing insights, commenting on others' posts, and participating in industry discussions.

Strategy: The 10-Minute Daily Networking Routine

- Share one relevant article or insight
- Comment on three posts in your network
- Connect with one new person in your industry

3. Join and participate in online communities

Engage with professional groups or forums related to your industry or interests.

Best Practice: Aim to add value to the community by sharing knowledge, asking thoughtful questions, and offering support to others.

4. Leverage virtual events and webinars

Join online events to broaden your knowledge and expand your network.

Technique: The Virtual Event Networking Plan

- Research speakers and attendees beforehand
- Prepare relevant questions or talking points
- Actively participate in Q&A sessions or chat discussions
- Follow up with new connections after the event.

5. Master the art of the virtual coffee chat

Use video calls to have one-on-one conversations with new or existing connections.

Best Practices:

- Suggest a specific date and time when reaching out
- Prepare talking points or questions ahead of time
- Keep the conversation to 20-30 minutes
- End with a clear next step or action item

Case Study: The Remote Networker

Alex, a marketing professional transitioning to remote work, initially struggled to maintain and expand his professional network. By implementing the strategies we've discussed, he was able to thrive in the virtual networking landscape:

1. Alex optimized his LinkedIn profile, clearly highlighting his skills and experience.
2. He committed to spending 10 minutes daily engaging on LinkedIn, sharing industry insights and commenting on others' posts.
3. Alex joined two professional marketing groups on LinkedIn and regularly participated in discussions.
4. He attended monthly virtual marketing webinars, actively participating in Q&A sessions.
5. Alex initiated virtual coffee chats with new connections he made through these activities.

Over six months, Alex expanded his professional network by 40%, landed two new freelance projects through his online connections, and was invited to speak at a virtual marketing conference.

Practical Exercise: The Virtual Communication Challenge

Over the next week, challenge yourself to enhance your digital communication skills:

Day 1-2: Email Etiquette

- Review your sent emails from the past week
- Identify areas for improvement based on the guidelines discussed
- Draft three emails using the BLUF method

Day 3-4: Social Media Presence

- Audit your social media profiles for consistency and professionalism
- Create and share two posts using the best practices discussed
- Interact with five posts from your network.

Day 5-6: Virtual Meeting Skills

- Prepare your virtual meeting environment using the checklist
- Practice looking at the camera and using nonverbal cues
- If possible, record yourself in a mock presentation and review for areas of improvement

Day 7: Online Networking

- Optimize your LinkedIn profile using the 3C's technique
- Reach out to three new connections for virtual coffee chats
- Research and join one professional online community related to your field

Remember, mastering digital communication is an ongoing process. Regular practice and reflection will help you continually improve your skills and adapt to evolving digital norms.

By implementing these strategies for email etiquette, social media best practices, virtual meetings, and online networking, you'll enhance your digital communication skills and expand your professional opportunities in our increasingly connected world.

6.2: Cross-Cultural Communication

In our increasingly globalized world, the ability to communicate effectively across cultures has become an essential skill. Whether you're working in a multinational corporation, studying abroad, or simply interacting with diverse communities in your daily life, understanding and navigating cultural differences is crucial for success.

This subchapter explores the intricacies of cross-cultural communication, focusing on two key areas: understanding cultural communication styles and building global relationships while avoiding cultural missteps. We'll delve into the nuances of how different cultures express themselves, interpret messages, and build relationships, providing you with the tools to become a more effective global communicator.

Throughout this discussion, we'll consider two main factors: cultural intelligence and adaptability. Cultural intelligence refers to the ability to recognize, understand, and effectively navigate cultural differences. Adaptability, on the other hand, is the skill of adjusting one's communication style and behavior to suit different cultural contexts.

By developing these skills, you'll be better equipped to:

- Recognize and appreciate diverse communication styles
- Avoid common cultural misunderstandings
- Build strong relationships across cultural boundaries
- Adapt your communication approach to various cultural contexts

We'll examine real-world examples, share practical strategies, and provide actionable advice to help you become a more culturally competent communicator. Remember, mastering cross-cultural communication is an ongoing journey that requires openness, empathy, and a willingness to learn from others.

As we explore this topic, keep in mind that while cultural generalizations can be useful starting points, every individual is unique. The goal is to develop a flexible approach that allows you to connect meaningfully with people from all backgrounds. Let's begin our exploration of cross-cultural communication, starting with understanding cultural communication styles.

6.2.1 : Understanding cultural communication styles

Effective cross-cultural communication begins with recognizing that different cultures have unique ways of expressing themselves, interpreting messages, and viewing the world. By understanding these differences, we can adapt our communication style to bridge cultural gaps and foster better understanding.

High-Context vs. Low-Context Communication

One fundamental distinction in cultural communication styles is the concept of high-context versus low-context communication, introduced by anthropologist Edward T. Hall.

1. High-Context Cultures

In high-context cultures, much of the message is implied rather than explicitly stated. These cultures rely heavily on nonverbal cues, shared experiences, and cultural context to convey meaning.

Examples of high-context cultures: Japan, China, Arab countries, and many Latin American countries.

Characteristics:

- Indirect communication
- Emphasis on nonverbal cues
- Relationship-focused
- Group-oriented decision making

2. Low-Context Cultures

Low-context cultures favor direct, explicit communication. Messages are expected to be clear and straightforward, with less reliance on context or implicit understanding.

Examples of low-context cultures: United States, Germany, Australia, and many Northern European countries.

Characteristics:

- Direct communication
- Focus on verbal messages
- Task-oriented
- Individual-focused decision making

Case Study: The Misunderstood Refusal

Sarah, an American businesswoman, was negotiating a deal with a Japanese company. When she proposed a timeline, her Japanese counterpart replied, "That could be difficult." Sarah interpreted this as a minor obstacle and continued pushing forward. However, the deal eventually fell through, leaving Sarah confused.

What Sarah didn't realize was that in Japanese culture, a high-context communication style, saying something is "difficult" often means "no." The Japanese executive was politely refusing the proposal, but Sarah, used to low-context communication, missed the subtle cue.

Lesson: When communicating across cultures, be aware of potential differences in directness and learn to read between the lines.

Direct vs. Indirect Communication

Building on the high-context vs. low-context distinction, it's important to understand the spectrum of direct and indirect communication styles.

1. Direct Communication

Cultures that favor direct communication value clarity and efficiency in conveying messages.

Characteristics:

- Explicit statements of needs, wants, and opinions
- Use of "I" statements
- Comfort with disagreement and confrontation

2. Indirect Communication

Cultures that prefer indirect communication often prioritize harmony and face-saving.

Characteristics:

- Use of hints, suggestions, and implications
- Avoidance of direct refusals or criticisms
- Emphasis on contextual clues and nonverbal communication

Strategies for Navigating Communication Styles:

1. Practice active listening

Pay attention not just to words, but also to tone, body language, and what isn't being said.

2. Ask clarifying questions

When in doubt, politely ask for clarification to ensure you've understood the message correctly.

3. Adapt your communication style

When interacting with people from different cultures, try to match their level of directness or indirectness.

4. Be patient

Cross-cultural communication often requires more time and effort to ensure mutual understanding.

Nonverbal Communication Across Cultures

Nonverbal cues play a crucial role in communication, but their meanings can vary significantly across cultures.

Key areas of nonverbal communication to consider:

1. Personal space

The comfortable distance between people during interactions varies by culture. For example, Middle Eastern cultures often stand closer during conversations than North Americans or Northern Europeans.

2. Eye contact

While direct eye contact is seen as a sign of honesty and attentiveness in many Western cultures, it can be perceived as disrespectful or confrontational in some Asian and African cultures.

3. Gestures

Common gestures can have vastly different meanings across cultures. The "thumbs up" sign, for instance, is positive in many Western countries but can be offensive in parts of the Middle East and West Africa.

4. Touch

The acceptability and meaning of touch in professional and social settings vary widely. Some cultures are more tactile, while others prefer minimal physical contact.

5. Facial expressions

While some expressions (like smiles) are universally recognized, their use and interpretation can differ. In some Asian cultures, for example, smiling might be used to mask discomfort or disagreement.

Best Practice: Develop a "Nonverbal Vocabulary"

When engaging with a new culture, research common nonverbal cues and their meanings. Create a mental (or physical) list of dos and don'ts to guide your interactions.

6.2.2 : Building Global Relationships and Avoiding Cultural Missteps

Successfully navigating cross-cultural communication goes beyond understanding different styles; it involves building meaningful relationships and avoiding potential pitfalls. Let's explore strategies for fostering strong global connections and sidestepping common cultural missteps.

Building Global Relationships

1. Cultivate Cultural Intelligence (CQ)

Cultural Intelligence is the ability to engage and work effectively across different cultures. Developing CQ involves four key components:

- CQ Drive: The motivation to learn about and engage with other cultures
- CQ Knowledge: Awareness of cultural differences and similarities
- CQ Strategy: The capacity to plan for multicultural interactions
- CQ Action: The capability to adapt behavior in cross-cultural situations

Exercise: CQ Self-Assessment

Rate yourself on a scale of 1-5 for each CQ component. Identify areas for improvement and create an action plan to enhance your cultural intelligence.

2. Practice Active Empathy

Go beyond simply recognizing cultural differences; try to understand the underlying values and beliefs that shape them.

Technique: The Cultural Perspective-Taking Exercise

When faced with a cross-cultural challenge:

1. Describe the situation from your perspective
2. Imagine and describe the situation from the other person's cultural perspective
3. Identify potential misunderstandings or conflicts
4. Brainstorm solutions that respect both cultural viewpoints

3. Build Trust Through Consistency and Respect

Trust is the foundation of any strong relationship, but the path to building trust can vary across cultures.

Best Practices:

- Be dependable and consistent in your words and actions
- Show a sincere interest in learning about other cultures
- Respect cultural norms and traditions, even if you don't fully understand them
- Be patient; trust-building may take longer in some cultures than others

4. Leverage Common Ground

While focusing on cultural differences is important, finding shared interests and experiences can help bridge cultural gaps.

Strategy: The Commonality Search

In cross-cultural interactions, actively look for:

- Shared professional interests
- Common hobbies or passions
- Similar life experiences
- Universal human values

Case Study: The Global Team Success Story

Maria, a project manager from Brazil, was tasked with leading a diverse team with members from India, Germany, and the United States. Initially, the team struggled with miscommunication and missed deadlines. Maria implemented several strategies to improve team dynamics:

1. She organized a virtual "cultural exchange" session where team members shared aspects of their cultures, fostering mutual understanding.

2. Maria adapted her communication style, being more direct with her German and American team members, while using a more relationship-focused approach with her Indian colleagues.

3. She established clear communication protocols, combining written summaries (for low-context communicators) with follow-up calls (for high-context communicators).

4. The team created a shared glossary of terms to ensure everyone had the same understanding of key concepts.

As a result, team cohesion improved significantly, and the project was completed successfully, on time and within budget.

Avoiding Cultural Missteps

Even with good intentions, cultural missteps can happen. Here are some strategies to reduce the risk:

1. Do Your Homework

Before engaging with a new culture, research basic etiquette, customs, and taboos.

Resource: Create a Cultural Cheat Sheet

For each new culture you interact with, note down:

- Appropriate greetings and forms of address
- Gift-giving customs
- Dining etiquette
- Business meeting norms
- Taboo topics or gestures

2. Avoid Stereotyping

While cultural generalizations can be useful starting points, avoid applying them rigidly to individuals.

Technique: The Individual Approach

- Start with cultural generalizations as a guide
- Observe the individual's behavior and communication style
- Adjust your approach based on the person, not just their cultural background

3. Be Mindful of Time Perceptions

Attitudes toward time, punctuality, and scheduling can vary significantly across cultures.

Examples:

- Monochronic cultures (e.g., Germany, USA) value punctuality and strict scheduling

- Polychronic cultures (e.g., Latin America, Middle East) have a more flexible view of time

Strategy: Time Expectation Alignment

When scheduling cross-cultural meetings or deadlines, explicitly discuss and agree on time expectations.

4. Navigate Language Barriers

When communicating in a non-native language, be patient and considerate.

Best Practices:

- Speak clearly and at a moderate pace
- Avoid idioms, slang, or colloquialisms
- Use visual aids when possible
- Confirm understanding by asking for summaries or paraphrasing

5. Apologize and Learn from Mistakes

If you do make a cultural misstep, apologize sincerely and use it as a learning opportunity.

Technique: The Cultural Mistake Reflection

When you make a cultural error:

1. Acknowledge the mistake

2. Apologize sincerely

3. Ask for clarification on the correct behavior

4. Thank the person for their understanding

5. Make a note to avoid the mistake in the future

Practical Exercise: The Cultural Communication Challenge

Over the next week, challenge yourself to enhance your cross-cultural communication skills:

Day 1-2: Cultural Style Awareness

- Recognize a culture that differs from your own
- Research its communication style (high/low context, direct/indirect)
- Practice adapting your communication style in a hypothetical scenario

Day 3-4: Nonverbal Communication

- Learn about nonverbal cues in your target culture
- Practice appropriate gestures, eye contact, and personal space
- If possible, watch films or videos from that culture to observe nonverbal communication

Day 5-6: Relationship Building

- Reach out to a colleague or acquaintance from a different cultural background
- Schedule a virtual coffee chat to learn more about their culture
- Engage in active listening and demonstrate empathy during the conversation.

Day 7: Reflection and Planning

- Reflect on what you've learned about cross-cultural communication
- Recognize areas where you can enhance your skills further
- Create an action plan for continued cross-cultural learning

Remember, becoming proficient in cross-cultural communication is a lifelong journey. Every interaction is a chance to develop and learn. By consistently applying these principles and remaining open to new experiences, you'll develop the skills to navigate our diverse global landscape with confidence and respect.

99

Chapter 7: Advanced Communication Skills

Picture yourself as a master sculptor, chiseling away at a block of marble to reveal a breathtaking masterpiece. Just as the sculptor refines their technique to create intricate details and evoke powerful emotions, so too can we hone our communication skills to craft messages that resonate, inspire, and drive action.

In this chapter, we'll delve into the realm of advanced communication, exploring techniques that elevate everyday interactions to art forms. We'll focus on two key factors that distinguish exceptional communicators: adaptability and emotional intelligence.

Adaptability allows us to tailor our message and style to various audiences and situations, ensuring our words hit their mark every time. Emotional intelligence, on the other hand, enables us to read between the lines, understand unspoken sentiments, and connect with others on a deeper level.

As we embark on this journey to communication mastery, remember that these skills are not innate talents, but rather abilities that can be developed and refined over time. With practice and dedication, you can transform your communication from functional to phenomenal.

We'll explore:

1. The power of storytelling in communication
2. Advanced listening techniques
3. Mastering nonverbal cues
4. Persuasion and influence strategies
5. Navigating difficult conversations

Each section will provide practical tips, real-world examples, and exercises to help you apply these concepts in your daily life. By the end of this chapter, you'll have a toolkit of advanced communication techniques at your disposal, ready to be deployed in personal and professional settings alike.

So, sharpen your communication tools and prepare to sculpt your words with precision and impact. Let's dive into the world of advanced communication skills and unlock your potential to connect, persuade, and inspire.

7.1: Emotional Intelligence in Communication

In the intricate dance of human interaction, emotional intelligence serves as the choreographer, guiding our steps and helping us move in harmony with others. This subchapter explores the crucial role of emotional intelligence in communication, focusing on two key aspects: recognizing and managing emotions, and adapting to different communication styles.

Emotional intelligence, or EQ, is the ability to recognize, utilize, and regulate our emotions in positive ways to reduce stress, communicate effectively, empathize with others, navigate challenges, and resolve conflicts. In the context of communication, EQ becomes a powerful tool that can transform our interactions, making them more meaningful, productive, and satisfying.

As we delve into this topic, we'll consider two main factors that influence emotional intelligence in communication: self-awareness and social awareness. Self-awareness involves recognizing our own emotions and understanding how they affect our behavior and communication. Social awareness, on the other hand, is about perceiving and understanding the emotions of others and how they influence interactions.

By developing these skills, you'll be better equipped to:

- Identify and manage your own emotional responses in various situations
- Acknowledge people' feelings and react accordingly
- Adapt your communication style to different individuals and contexts
- Build stronger, more empathetic relationships in both personal and professional settings

Throughout this discussion, we'll explore practical strategies, real-life examples, and exercises to help you enhance your emotional intelligence and apply it to your daily communications. Remember, improving your EQ is an ongoing process that requires practice and patience. The goal is to become more attuned to both your own emotions and those of others, allowing for more effective and empathetic communication.

Let's begin our exploration of emotional intelligence in communication, starting with recognizing and managing emotions in yourself and others.

7.1.1 : Recognizing and managing emotions in yourself and others

Emotional intelligence starts with self-awareness—the ability to identify and understand your own emotions. This skill forms the foundation for effective communication, as it allows you to manage your reactions and choose appropriate responses in various situations.

Self-Awareness: The First Step

Developing self-awareness involves paying attention to your emotional states, their triggers, and how they influence your behavior and communication. Here are some strategies to enhance your self-awareness:

1. Practice mindfulness

Make time to check in with yourself every day. Without passing judgment, pay attention to your feelings, ideas, and bodily experiences.

Exercise: The Emotion Log

For one week, keep a daily log of your emotions. Note:

- The emotion you're feeling
- What triggered it
- How you expressed or managed it
- The impact on your communication

2. Identify your emotional triggers

Recognize situations, people, or events that consistently evoke strong emotional responses in you.

3. Understand your emotional patterns

Notice how your emotions typically unfold. Do you tend to react quickly, or do your emotions build up over time?

Case Study: The Frustrated Manager

Sarah, a marketing manager, often found herself snapping at her team during high-stress periods. By practicing self-awareness, she realized that tight deadlines triggered feelings of anxiety, which she then projected onto her team as irritation. Once she recognized this pattern, Sarah was able to implement stress-management techniques and communicate her concerns more constructively with her team.

Managing Your Emotions

Once you've identified your emotions, the next step is learning to manage them effectively. This doesn't mean suppressing your feelings, but rather expressing them in constructive ways.

Strategies for emotion management:

1. Practice the pause

When you feel a strong emotion arising, take a moment before responding. This brief pause can help you choose a more appropriate reaction.

2. Use reframing techniques

Look at the situation from different perspectives to gain a more balanced view.

3. Engage in self-care

Regular exercise, adequate sleep, and healthy eating can improve your overall emotional resilience.

4. Develop a personal calming routine

This could involve deep breathing, counting to ten, or visualizing a peaceful scene.

Recognizing Emotions in Others

Social awareness, the ability to recognize and understand others' emotions, is crucial for effective communication. Here are some ways to enhance this skill:

1. Pay attention to nonverbal cues

Body language, facial expressions, and tone of voice often convey more about a person's emotional state than their words.

2. Practice active listening

Focus fully on the speaker, acknowledging their message and reflecting back what you've heard to ensure understanding.

3. Develop empathy

Try to put yourself in the other person's shoes and imagine how they might be feeling.

Exercise: The Empathy Challenge

In your next three conversations:

1. Focus on identifying the other person's emotional state

2. Consider what might be causing those emotions

3. Reflect on how their emotional state influences the interaction

Responding to Others' Emotions

Once you've recognized others' emotions, responding appropriately is key to effective communication.

Strategies for emotion management:

1. Practice the pause

When you feel a strong emotion arising, take a moment before responding. This brief pause can help you choose a more appropriate reaction.

2. Use reframing techniques

Look at the situation from different perspectives to gain a more balanced view.

3. Engage in self-care

Regular exercise, adequate sleep, and healthy eating can improve your overall emotional resilience.

4. Develop a personal calming routine

This could involve deep breathing, counting to ten, or visualizing a peaceful scene.

Recognizing Emotions in Others

Social awareness, the ability to recognize and understand others' emotions, is crucial for effective communication.

Here are some ways to enhance this skill:

1. Pay attention to nonverbal cues

A person's emotional state is often conveyed more through body language, facial expressions, and tone of voice than through words.

2. Practice active listening

Focus fully on the speaker, acknowledging their message and reflecting back what you've heard to ensure understanding.

3. Develop empathy

Try to put yourself in the other person's shoes and imagine how they might be feeling.

Exercise: The Empathy Challenge

In your next three conversations:

1. Focus on identifying the other person's emotional state

2. Consider what might be causing those emotions

3. Reflect on how their emotional state influences the interaction

Responding to Others' Emotions

Once you've recognized others' emotions, responding appropriately is key to effective communication.

Strategies for emotional responsiveness:

1. Validate feelings

Acknowledge the other person's emotions without necessarily agreeing with their perspective.

2. Use "I" statements

Without placing blame or offering criticism, communicate your own needs and feelings.

3. Offer support

Ask how you can help or what the other person needs.

4. Practice compassionate assertiveness

Express your own needs and boundaries while respecting others' emotions.

Real-life Example: The Empathetic Leader

John, a team leader in a tech company, noticed that one of his usually enthusiastic employees, Mark, seemed withdrawn and less productive. Instead of immediately addressing the performance issue, John approached Mark with concern:

John: "Mark, I've noticed you've seemed a little down lately. Is everything okay?"

Mark: "I'm fine, just a bit stressed."

John: "I understand stress can be tough. Is there anything specific that's bothering you, or anything I can do to help?"

Mark: "Actually, I've been worried about my mom's health. It's been hard to focus."

John: "I'm sorry to hear that. That must be really difficult. Let's talk about how we can adjust your workload to give you some space to deal with this."

By recognizing Mark's emotional state and responding with empathy, John was able to address the underlying issue and support his employee, likely improving both Mark's well-being and his productivity in the long run.

7.1.2: Adapting to different communication styles

Just as people have different personalities, they also have varying communication styles. The ability to recognize and adapt to these different styles is a crucial aspect of emotional intelligence in communication.

Understanding Communication Styles

While individual communication styles can vary widely, they often fall into four main categories:

1. Analytical: Focuses on data, facts, and logical thinking

2. Intuitive: Prefers big-picture thinking and abstract ideas

3. Functional: Emphasizes processes, details, and step-by-step plans

4. Personal: Prioritizes emotions, relationships, and personal experiences

Recognizing these styles can help you tailor your communication approach for more effective interactions.

Exercise: Identify Your Style

Reflect on your typical communication patterns. Which of the four styles do you most closely align with? How could this affect your interactions with others?

Adapting Your Communication

The key to effective communication across different styles is flexibility. Here are strategies to adapt to each style:

1. For Analytical Communicators:

- Back up your points with data and evidence
- Be clear and specific in your language
- Avoid emotional appeals

2. For Intuitive Communicators:

- Begin with the big picture before getting into the details
- Use metaphors and analogies to clarify concepts

- Be open to brainstorming and exploring new ideas

3. For Functional Communicators:

- Provide clear, step-by-step explanations
- Be prepared with specific examples and details
- Focus on practical applications and outcomes

4. For Personal Communicators:

- Build rapport before discussing business
- Share personal experiences and stories
- Demonstrate empathy and actively listen to their concerns

Case Study: The Cross-Functional Team

A product development team consisting of Sarah (analytical), Mike (intuitive), Lisa (functional), and Tom (personal) was struggling with communication issues. Their project manager, Alex, recognized the need to adapt his communication style for each team member:

- With Sarah, Alex provided detailed data on project metrics and timelines.
- For Mike, Alex started meetings with an overview of the project vision before discussing specifics.
- When speaking with Lisa, Alex broke down complex tasks into clear, actionable steps.
- With Tom, Alex took time to check in personally before diving into work-related discussions.

By adapting his approach, Alex improved team communication and collaboration, leading to a successful project outcome.

Bridging Communication Gaps

Even with adaptation, misunderstandings can occur.

Here are strategies to bridge communication gaps:

1. Practice active listening

Ensure you fully understand the other person's message before responding.

2. Ask clarifying questions

Don't hesitate to seek clarification if something is unclear.

3. Paraphrase and summarize

Repeat or paraphrase what you've heard to confirm understanding.

4. Be open to feedback

Encourage others to let you know if your communication style isn't working for them.

5. Seek common ground

Look for shared goals or interests to build rapport across different styles.

Practical Exercise: Style Switching

Over the next week, practice adapting your communication style:

Day 1-2: Identify

- Observe the communication styles of people you interact with regularly
- Note how their style differs from yours

Day 3-4: Adapt

- Choose one person with a different style
- Consciously adapt your communication approach with them
- Note the results of this adaptation

Day 5-6: Reflect

- Consider which adaptations were most effective
- Identify areas where you struggled to adapt

Day 7: Plan

- Based on your observations, create a plan for improving your style flexibility
- Set specific goals for adapting your communication in future interactions

Remember, becoming adept at recognizing and managing emotions, as well as adapting to different communication styles, is an ongoing process. Every engagement offers a chance to hone these abilities. By consistently applying emotional intelligence principles to your communication, you'll build stronger relationships, resolve conflicts more effectively, and navigate complex social situations with greater ease.

7.2: The Ethics of Communication

In the vast landscape of human interaction, communication serves as the bridge that connects individuals, communities, and cultures. However, this bridge is only as strong as the ethical foundations upon which it is built. The ethics of communication form the bedrock of trust, respect, and understanding in our personal and professional relationships.

This subchapter delves into the crucial role that ethics plays in effective communication. We'll explore two main factors that shape ethical communication: integrity and responsibility. Integrity in communication involves being truthful, transparent, and consistent in our words and actions. Responsibility, on the other hand, refers to the conscious choice to use our communication skills in ways that benefit others and society as a whole.

As we explore this subject, we'll look at:

1. The importance of honesty and integrity in communication

2. The responsible use of persuasion techniques

These elements are not just abstract concepts but practical tools that can enhance the quality of our interactions and the impact of our messages. By understanding and applying ethical principles in our communication, we can build stronger relationships, foster trust, and create positive change in our personal and professional spheres.

Throughout this discussion, we'll explore real-world examples, practical strategies, and thought-provoking exercises to help you integrate ethical communication practices into your daily life. Remember, ethical communication is not about perfection, but about continuous improvement and conscious effort.

Let's embark on this journey to discover how ethics can transform our communication from merely effective to truly impactful and meaningful.

7.2.1: Honesty and integrity in communication

Honesty and integrity form the cornerstone of ethical communication. They are the foundation upon which trust is built and maintained in all our interactions. But what do these terms really mean in the context of communication?

Honesty in communication refers to the truthfulness of our words and the accuracy of the information we share. It involves being open about our thoughts, feelings, and intentions, even when it might be uncomfortable or disadvantageous to do so.

Integrity, on the other hand, goes beyond mere honesty. It encompasses consistency between our words and actions, adherence to our values, and taking responsibility for our communication choices. Integrity in communication means that our words align with our beliefs and behaviors, creating a coherent and trustworthy persona.

The Importance of Honesty and Integrity

Honest and integral communication offers numerous benefits:

1. Builds trust: When people know they can rely on your words, they're more likely to trust and respect you.

2. Enhances credibility: Consistent honesty boosts your reputation and makes your messages more persuasive.

3. Fosters open dialogue: When you're honest, others are more likely to reciprocate, leading to more meaningful conversations.

4. Reduces stress: Being truthful eliminates the need to keep track of lies or half-truths, reducing mental burden.

Case Study: The Transparent CEO

Sarah, the CEO of a mid-sized tech company, faced a challenging situation when a major product launch failed. Instead of trying to cover up the failure or shift blame, she chose to be transparent with her employees and stakeholders. She sent out a company-wide email explaining what went wrong, taking responsibility for the missteps, and outlining a plan to learn from the experience.

This honest approach initially caused some concern among investors, but in the long run, it strengthened the company culture, improved employee morale, and even attracted new talent who valued the company's commitment to integrity.

Practical Strategies for Honest Communication

1. Practice self-awareness

Before communicating, take a moment to check in with yourself. Are you being fully truthful? Are there any biases or hidden agendas influencing your message?

2. Use "I" statements

When expressing opinions or feelings, make it clear that they are your own. For example, "I feel frustrated when..." instead of "You always..."

3. Admit mistakes and uncertainties

If you've made a mistake or are unsure about something, acknowledge it openly. This shows humility and builds trust.

4. Provide context

When sharing information, give enough context to ensure it's not misleading, even if unintentionally.

5. Respectfully disagree

When you don't agree with someone, express your disagreement honestly but respectfully. Avoid personal attacks or dismissive language.

Exercise: The Honesty Audit

For one week, keep a communication journal. At the end of each day, reflect on your interactions and ask yourself:

1. Were there any moments when I was less than fully honest? Why?

2. Did I avoid any difficult truths? How could I have addressed them more directly?

3. Were my words consistent with my actions and values?

4. How can I improve my honesty and integrity in similar situations in the future?

Challenges to Honesty and Integrity

While the benefits of honest communication are clear, there are situations where being completely truthful can be challenging or even seem counterproductive. Let's explore some of these scenarios:

1. White lies: Small untruths told to avoid hurting someone's feelings or to smooth social interactions.

2. Confidentiality: When you have information that you're not at liberty to share.

3. Competitive advantage: In business or negotiation settings where revealing all information might be disadvantageous.

4. Cultural differences: In some cultures, indirect communication is valued over blunt honesty.

Navigating these challenges requires careful consideration and often a balance between honesty and other ethical principles like kindness or respect for privacy.

Example: The Diplomatic Manager

John, a team manager, was asked by a colleague about the performance of one of his team members who was being considered for a promotion. While the team member had some strengths, John was aware of some significant weaknesses that would make them unsuitable for the new role.

John chose to be honest about both the strengths and weaknesses, framing his feedback constructively: "Sarah has excellent project management skills and consistently meets deadlines. However, she's still developing her leadership abilities and might benefit from more experience before taking on a senior role."

By being truthful while also being considerate in his phrasing, John maintained his integrity and provided valuable information without unnecessarily damaging his team member's reputation.

Persuasion is a powerful tool in communication, capable of inspiring action, changing minds, and shaping behaviors. However, with great power comes great responsibility. The ethical use of persuasion techniques is crucial to maintain trust, respect, and fairness in our interactions.

Understanding Persuasion

Persuasion involves the intentional effort to influence someone's attitudes, beliefs, or behaviors. It's a skill used in various contexts, from marketing and politics to personal relationships and professional settings.

Key persuasion techniques include:

1. Reciprocity: Giving something to encourage a return favor

2. Social proof: Showing that others are doing or believing something

3. Authority: Leveraging expertise or credibility

4. Scarcity: Highlighting limited availability or exclusive opportunities

5. Consistency: Encouraging people to act in line with their past actions or statements

6. Liking: Building rapport and finding common ground

The Ethics of Persuasion

Ethical persuasion involves using these techniques responsibly, with consideration for the well-being and autonomy of others. Here are some principles for ethical persuasion:

1. Truthfulness: Ensure all information used in persuasion is accurate and not misleading.

2. Transparency: Be open about your intentions and any potential conflicts of interest.

3. Respect for autonomy: Allow others to make informed decisions without undue pressure.

4. Fairness: Avoid exploiting vulnerabilities or using manipulative tactics.

5. Beneficence: Aim for outcomes that benefit both parties, not just yourself.

Case Study: The Ethical Marketer

Lisa, a marketing manager for a health supplement company, was tasked with creating a campaign for a new product. The product had shown some positive results in preliminary studies, but the research wasn't conclusive.

Instead of exaggerating the benefits or using fear tactics, Lisa chose to focus on transparently communicating the known facts. She included information about the ongoing research, encouraged customers to consult with healthcare providers, and offered a satisfaction guarantee.

This approach not only aligned with ethical principles but also built long-term trust with customers, leading to sustained sales and positive word-of-mouth recommendations.

Strategies for Responsible Persuasion

1. Know your audience

Understand the needs, values, and concerns of your audience to tailor your message appropriately.

2. Use evidence-based arguments

Support your points with credible data and examples.

3. Present balanced information

Acknowledge potential drawbacks or limitations of your position.

4. Avoid emotional manipulation

While it's okay to appeal to emotions, avoid exploiting fears or insecurities.

5. Respect boundaries

If someone clearly isn't interested, respect their decision and don't push further.

6. Offer choices

Present options rather than trying to force a single course of action.

Exercise: Ethical Persuasion Analysis

Choose a recent advertisement or persuasive message you've encountered. Analyze it based on the following questions:

1. What persuasion techniques does it use?

2. Is the information presented truthfully and transparently?

3. Does it respect the audience's autonomy?

4. Are there any ethical concerns with the approach?

5. How could the message be modified to be more ethically sound while still being effective?

Challenges in Ethical Persuasion

Even with the best intentions, ethical persuasion can face challenges:

1. Competing interests: Balancing personal or organizational goals with ethical considerations.

2. Unclear outcomes: The long-term effects of persuasion may not always be predictable.

3. Cultural differences: What's considered ethical persuasion may vary across cultures.

4. Power imbalances: When there's a significant power difference between the persuader and the audience.

Navigating these challenges requires ongoing reflection, openness to feedback, and a commitment to ethical principles.

Example: The Ethical Negotiator

Sarah, a freelance designer, was negotiating a contract with a potential client. The client was offering a rate below Sarah's usual fee, citing budget constraints. Sarah knew the client's company had recently received a large investment.

Instead of using this information to pressure the client or make accusations, Sarah chose a transparent approach: "I understand budget concerns are important. Given the scope of the project, my standard rate is [X]. I believe this reflects the value I can bring, especially considering your company's recent growth. However, I'm open to discussing how we can structure the project to meet both our needs."

By being honest about her rates, acknowledging the client's position, and offering flexibility, Sarah maintained her integrity while still advocating for her worth.

In conclusion, ethical communication, rooted in honesty, integrity, and responsible persuasion, is not just a moral imperative but a practical approach to building lasting relationships and achieving meaningful outcomes. By integrating these principles into our daily interactions, we can elevate the quality of our communication and contribute to a more trustworthy and respectful society.

Chapter 8: The Future of Communication

As we stand on the cusp of a new era, the landscape of human interaction is undergoing a dramatic transformation. The future of communication is not just approaching, it's already unfolding before our eyes. This chapter invites you to explore the cutting-edge developments and emerging trends that are reshaping the way we connect, share ideas, and build relationships.

Two main factors are driving this communication revolution:

1. Technological advancements

2. Shifting societal norms

These forces are intertwining to create a communication ecosystem that is more dynamic, immersive, and interconnected than ever before.

Technological advancements are expanding the limits of what is possible. From artificial intelligence that can engage in human-like conversations to virtual reality platforms that transport us to shared digital spaces, the tools at our disposal are becoming increasingly sophisticated. These innovations are not just changing how we communicate, but also redefining the very nature of interaction itself.

Simultaneously, our societal norms are evolving. The global pandemic has accelerated the adoption of remote work and digital socializing, blurring the lines between personal and professional communication. Generational shifts are bringing new expectations for authenticity, immediacy, and inclusivity in our exchanges.

As we delve into this chapter, we'll explore how these factors are shaping the future of communication. We'll examine emerging technologies, discuss their potential impacts, and consider the ethical implications of these advancements. We'll also look at how changing social dynamics are influencing communication styles and preferences.

Whether you're a tech enthusiast, a business professional, or simply curious about the future, this chapter offers insights into the communication landscape that awaits us. By understanding these trends, we can better prepare ourselves to navigate and thrive in the evolving world of human interaction.

Prepare to embark on a journey into the future of communication—a future that is both exhilarating and challenging, filled with unprecedented opportunities for connection and collaboration.

8.1: Embracing Technological Changes

In the ever-evolving landscape of communication, technological advancements stand as both a challenge and an opportunity. This subchapter explores the transformative power of technology in shaping how we connect, share information, and interact with one another.

The swift pace of technological change can be both exciting and daunting. From artificial intelligence to virtual reality, new tools and platforms are constantly emerging, reshaping our communication landscape. These innovations offer exciting possibilities for more efficient, engaging, and personalized interactions. However, they also present challenges as we adapt to new ways of connecting and expressing ourselves.

Two main factors are driving this technological revolution in communication:

1. The exponential growth of computing power and data processing capabilities

2. The increasing integration of technology into our daily lives

As we navigate this changing terrain, it's crucial to understand not only the capabilities of these new technologies but also their implications for our personal and professional lives.

In this subchapter, we'll explore:

1. How AI and automation are reshaping communication

2. Strategies for staying relevant in a rapidly changing landscape

By examining these topics, we'll gain insights into the future of communication and develop strategies to thrive in this new era. Whether you're a tech enthusiast or someone who feels intimidated by new technologies, this exploration will provide valuable perspectives on embracing technological changes in communication.

Let's dive into the world of AI, automation, and digital transformation, and discover how we can harness these tools to enhance our communication skills and stay ahead in an increasingly tech-driven world.

8.1.1 : How AI and automation are reshaping communication

Artificial Intelligence (AI) and automation are no longer confined to science fiction; they're actively reshaping our communication landscape. These technologies are transforming how we interact with each other, with businesses, and with information itself. Let's explore the ways AI and automation are influencing various aspects of communication.

1. Personalized Communication

AI algorithms are enabling unprecedented levels of personalization in communication. From tailored email marketing campaigns to personalized content recommendations, AI is helping to deliver messages that resonate with individual preferences and behaviors.

Case Study: Netflix's Recommendation System

Netflix leverages AI to analyze viewing habits and deliver personalized content recommendations. This not only enhances user experience but also communicates the platform's value to each subscriber uniquely. The system considers factors like viewing history, time of day, and even device type to suggest content that's most likely to appeal to each user.

2. Language Processing and Translation

Natural Language Processing (NLP) technologies are breaking down language barriers and making cross-cultural communication easier than ever.

Example: Google Translate

Google Translate's AI-powered system can now translate between over 100 languages in real-time. This technology is not only useful for travelers but also for businesses operating in global markets, enabling smoother communication across language barriers.

3. Chatbots and Virtual Assistants

AI-powered chatbots and virtual assistants are revolutionizing customer service and personal productivity.

Personal Anecdote: A Helpful Hotel Chatbot

During a recent trip, I encountered a hotel chatbot that could answer questions about amenities, make reservations for the hotel restaurant, and even process room service orders. The 24/7 availability and quick responses made my stay much more convenient and enjoyable.

4. Predictive Text and Writing Assistance

AI is helping us communicate more efficiently by predicting what we want to say and offering writing suggestions.

Example: Grammarly

Grammarly uses AI to not only correct grammar and spelling, but also to suggest improvements in style and tone. This tool helps users communicate more effectively across various platforms, from emails to social media posts.

5. Data-Driven Insights

AI and automation are enabling businesses to gather and analyze vast amounts of communication data, leading to more informed strategies.

Case Study: Social Media Sentiment Analysis

Many companies now use AI-powered tools to analyze social media conversations about their brand. This helps them understand public sentiment, respond to customer concerns quickly, and tailor their communication strategies accordingly.

Challenges and Ethical Considerations

While AI and automation bring several benefits, they also come with challenges:

1. Privacy concerns: The collection and analysis of communication data raise questions about privacy and data security.

2. Job displacement: As AI takes over certain communication tasks, some jobs may become obsolete.

3. Authenticity: There's a growing concern about the authenticity of AI-generated content and the potential for deepfakes.

4. Overreliance on technology: Excessive dependence on AI for communication might lead to a decline in human interpersonal skills.

Exercise: AI in Your Daily Communication

Take a moment to reflect on your daily communication:

1. List three ways AI or automation assists your communication (e.g., autocorrect, email filters).

2. Identify one area where you think AI could improve your communication efficiency.

3. Consider potential drawbacks of relying on AI in this area.

8.1.2: Staying relevant in a rapidly changing landscape

As technology continues to reshape communication, staying relevant requires adaptability, continuous learning, and a willingness to embrace change. Here are strategies to help you navigate and thrive in this evolving landscape:

1. Embrace Lifelong Learning

The key to staying relevant is committing to ongoing education and skill development.

Example: The Adaptable Marketing Professional

Sarah, a marketing professional with 20 years of experience, found her skills becoming outdated as digital marketing took center stage. Instead of resisting the change, she enrolled in online courses on digital marketing, social media strategy, and data analytics. Her willingness to learn new skills not only kept her relevant but also led to a promotion as she became the go-to person for digital initiatives in her company.

Actionable Tip: Set aside time each week to learn about new communication technologies. This may include reading industry blogs, enrolling in online courses, or attending webinars.

2. Develop a Growth Mindset

Approach technological changes with curiosity and openness rather than fear or resistance.

Personal Anecdote: From Technophobe to Tech Enthusiast

I used to dread learning new software or platforms. However, I decided to change my mindset and approach each new tool as an opportunity to enhance my skills. This shift in perspective has not only made me more adaptable but also more valuable in my professional life.

3. Balance Technology with Human Touch

While embracing new technologies, don't forget the importance of human connection in communication.

Case Study: The Human-Centric Call Center

A large telecommunications company implemented AI-powered chatbots to handle customer inquiries. However, they also trained their human representatives in empathy and complex problem-solving. This balanced approach led to higher customer satisfaction as routine queries were handled efficiently by AI, while more complex or emotionally charged issues were addressed with human empathy and expertise.

4. Stay Informed About Industry Trends

Keep abreast of emerging technologies and trends in communication to anticipate changes and adapt proactively.

Actionable Tip: Follow industry leaders, join professional groups on social media, and attend conferences or webinars to stay informed about the latest developments in communication technology.

5. Develop Transferable Skills

Focus on developing skills that remain valuable regardless of technological changes, such as critical thinking, creativity, and emotional intelligence.

Example: The Versatile Content Creator

Alex, a content creator, focused on developing strong storytelling skills. As new platforms emerged – from blogs to social media to podcasts – Alex was able to adapt his storytelling techniques to each medium, remaining relevant and successful across changing technological landscapes.

6. Experiment with New Tools and Platforms

Don't be afraid to try new communication tools and platforms, even if they're outside your comfort zone.

Exercise: Technology Exploration Challenge

Each month, choose a new communication tool or platform you're unfamiliar with. Spend time exploring its features and trying to incorporate it into your personal or professional communication. Reflect on what you've learned and how it might be useful in your communication strategy.

7. Cultivate Digital Literacy

Understand not just how to use new technologies, but also their implications and potential impacts.

Case Study: The Media-Savvy Educator

A high school teacher recognized the need to educate students about digital literacy. She developed a curriculum that not only taught students how to use various digital communication tools but also how to critically evaluate online information, understand digital privacy, and navigate the ethical considerations of online communication. This approach prepared students to be responsible digital citizens in a rapidly changing world.

8. Network and Collaborate

Build connections with people who have diverse skill sets and perspectives on communication technology.

Actionable Tip: Join online communities or local groups focused on communication technology. Participate in discussions, share your insights, and learn from others.

9. Maintain Work-Life Balance

As communication technologies blur the lines between work and personal life, it's crucial to set boundaries and maintain a healthy balance.

Personal Anecdote: The Importance of Digital Detox

I found myself constantly connected, checking emails and messages at all hours. Recognizing the negative impact on my well-being, I implemented a "digital sunset" – a time each evening when I disconnect from all devices. This practice has improved my personal relationships and overall quality of life, reminding me that effective communication also involves knowing when to disconnect.

As we navigate the ever-changing landscape of communication technology, remember that the goal is not to chase every new trend, but to thoughtfully adapt and integrate technologies that enhance our ability to connect, share ideas, and collaborate effectively. By staying curious, flexible, and grounded in fundamental communication skills, we can remain relevant and effective communicators in any technological era.

8.2: Predicting Communication Trends

As we navigate the ever-evolving landscape of communication, anticipating future trends becomes crucial for personal and professional success. This subchapter delves into the art and science of predicting communication trends, offering insights into the forces shaping our future interactions.

Predicting trends in communication is not merely an exercise in speculation; it's a strategic approach to understanding and preparing for the changes that will impact how we connect, collaborate, and share information. By examining current patterns and emerging technologies, we can gain valuable foresight into the communication landscape of tomorrow.

Two main factors drive the evolution of communication trends:

1. Technological advancements

2. Shifting societal needs and behaviors

These factors intertwine, creating a dynamic ecosystem where new communication tools and practices emerge, evolve, and sometimes fade away.

In this subchapter, we'll explore:

1. Future trends in work and social communication

2. Strategies for preparing for the next wave of digital communication tools

By examining these topics, we'll equip ourselves with the knowledge and skills needed to adapt to and thrive in the changing communication landscape. Whether you're a business leader, a technology enthusiast, or simply someone interested in staying ahead of the curve, this exploration will provide valuable insights into the future of communication.

Let's embark on this journey of discovery, exploring the trends that will shape how we connect and communicate in the years to come. Through this exploration, we'll not only gain understanding but also develop the adaptability needed to navigate the exciting future of communication.

8.2.1: Future trends in work and social communication

As we peer into the future of communication, several trends are emerging that promise to reshape how we interact in both professional and personal spheres. Let's explore these trends and their potential impacts on our daily lives.

1. Immersive Virtual Environments

Virtual and augmented reality technologies are set to transform how we work and socialize, creating more immersive and engaging communication experiences.

Case Study: Virtual Office Spaces

TechCo, a forward-thinking software company, has implemented a virtual office using VR technology. Employees can "walk" into meeting rooms, collaborate on virtual whiteboards, and even have casual conversations in virtual break rooms. This setup has increased engagement among remote teams and fostered a sense of presence that was previously lacking in video calls.

2. AI-Powered Communication Assistants

Artificial Intelligence will play an increasingly significant role in facilitating and enhancing our communications.

Example: Advanced Email Management

Imagine an AI assistant that not only sorts your emails but also drafts responses based on your communication style, schedules meetings, and even provides summaries of lengthy email threads. Such tools are already in development and will likely become commonplace in the near future.

3. Hyper-Personalized Content Delivery

Communication will become increasingly tailored to individual preferences and contexts.

Personal Anecdote: The Adaptive News Feed

Recently, I started using a news app that learns from my reading habits. Over time, it began presenting articles not just based on my interests, but also considering my mood, the time of day, and even my location. This level of personalization made my news consumption more relevant and engaging.

4. Seamless Language Translation

Real-time translation technologies will continue to improve, breaking down language barriers in both professional and social settings.

Example: Universal Translators in Business Meetings

Multinational corporations are beginning to use earpieces that provide real-time translation during meetings. This technology allows for more inclusive and efficient global collaboration, enabling team members to communicate in their native languages while understanding each other perfectly.

5. Holographic Communications

While still in its early stages, holographic technology holds the promise of making remote communications feel more lifelike and present.

Case Study: Holographic Conferencing

A major tech company recently demonstrated a prototype for holographic conferencing. Participants could see life-sized, three-dimensional representations of each other, creating a sense of presence that goes beyond traditional video calls.

6. Emotion Recognition in Digital Communication

Advanced AI algorithms will be able to detect and interpret emotions in digital communications, adding a new layer of understanding to text-based interactions.

Example: Empathetic Customer Service Chatbots

Future customer service chatbots may be able to detect frustration or confusion in a customer's messages and adjust their responses accordingly, providing a more empathetic and effective service experience.

7. Decentralized Social Networks

With growing concerns about data privacy and platform control, decentralized social networks may gain popularity.

Case Study: The Rise of Mastodon

Mastodon, a decentralized social network, has been gaining traction as an alternative to traditional social media platforms. It allows users to create their own communities with their own rules, offering more control over personal data and content moderation.

8. Augmented Reality in Everyday Communication

AR technology will increasingly overlay digital information onto our physical world, enhancing our daily interactions.

Personal Anecdote: AR-Enhanced Networking

At a recent conference, I used an AR app that displayed attendees' names and brief bios when I looked at them through my smartphone camera. This technology made networking much more efficient and less awkward, as I could quickly recall important information about the people I was meeting.

Challenges and Considerations

While these trends offer exciting possibilities, they also present challenges:

1. Digital fatigue: As communication becomes more immersive and constant, managing screen time and maintaining work-life balance will be crucial.

2. Privacy concerns: More personalized and AI-driven communication raises questions about data privacy and security.

3. Authenticity: As AI becomes more involved in our communications, maintaining authentic human connections may become a challenge.

4. Digital divide: As communication technologies advance, ensuring equal access and preventing a widening gap between tech-savvy and less tech-savvy individuals will be important.

Exercise: Trend Impact Analysis

1. List three communication trends mentioned above that you think will have the biggest impact on your life or work.

2. For each trend, write down one potential benefit and one potential challenge.

3. Brainstorm how you might prepare for or adapt to these changes in your personal or professional life.

8.2.2 :Preparing for the next wave of digital communication tools

As we stand on the brink of a new era in digital communication, being prepared for the next wave of tools and technologies is crucial. Here are strategies to help you stay ahead of the curve and make the most of emerging communication tools:

1. Cultivate Digital Adaptability

Developing a mindset of digital adaptability is key to navigating the rapidly changing landscape of communication tools.

Personal Anecdote: The Adaptable Manager

When my company introduced a new project management platform, I initially struggled with the change. However, by approaching it with an open mind and dedicating time to learn its features, I not only adapted quickly but also discovered ways to improve our team's workflow. This experience taught me the value of embracing new tools rather than resisting change.

Actionable Tip: Set aside time each month to explore a new digital communication tool, even if it's not immediately relevant to your work. This practice will help you build adaptability and keep you aware of emerging trends.

2. Focus on Core Communication Skills

While tools may change, fundamental communication skills remain crucial.

Example: The Power of Active Listening

Despite advances in AI-powered communication tools, the ability to listen actively and empathize remains a uniquely human skill. Professionals who excel in these areas will always have an edge, regardless of the technology they're using.

3. Stay Informed About Emerging Technologies

Keeping abreast of technological developments will help you anticipate and prepare for changes in communication tools.

Case Study: The Forward-Thinking HR Department

An HR department at a large corporation made it a policy to have team members regularly report on new communication technologies. This practice allowed them to be early adopters of a virtual reality onboarding program, which significantly improved the experience for new hires and set the company apart as an innovative employer.

4. Develop a Learning Network

Build a network of individuals who are passionate about communication technology to share insights and learn collaboratively.

Actionable Tip: Join online communities or local meetups focused on communication technology. Engage in discussions, share your experiences, and learn from others who are exploring new tools and trends.

5. Experiment with Beta Versions and New Platforms

Don't be afraid to try out new communication tools in their early stages.

Personal Anecdote: Early Adoption of Slack

I joined the beta testing program for Slack when it was first launched. By familiarizing myself with the platform early on, I was able to lead its implementation in my organization when we decided to adopt it, smoothing the transition for my colleagues.

6. Prioritize Data Privacy and Security

As communication tools become more advanced, understanding and prioritizing data privacy and security becomes increasingly important.

Example: The Importance of End-to-End Encryption

When choosing new communication tools, prioritize those that offer robust security features like end-to-end encryption. This not only protects sensitive information but also builds trust with clients and colleagues.

7. Balance High-Tech with High-Touch

While embracing new technologies, remember the importance of human connection in communication.

Case Study: The Hybrid Approach to Customer Service

A retail company implemented an AI chatbot for initial customer inquiries but trained their human representatives to handle more complex or emotionally charged issues. This balanced approach led to higher customer satisfaction and more efficient use of human resources.

8. Develop Cross-Platform Fluency

As the number of communication platforms increases, the ability to navigate multiple tools seamlessly becomes crucial.

Exercise: Platform Exploration Challenge

1. List all the communication platforms you currently use (e.g., email, Slack, Zoom, etc.).

2. Identify one platform you're not familiar with but that's gaining popularity in your industry.

3. Spend a week exploring this new platform, learning its features and how it compares to tools you already use.

4. Reflect on how this new tool might complement or replace your existing communication methods.

9. Embrace Continuous Learning

The rapid pace of technological change means that learning must be an ongoing process.

Actionable Tip: Set up a "learning hour" each week dedicated to exploring new communication tools or improving your skills with existing ones. This could involve watching tutorials, reading articles, or experimenting with new features.

10. Anticipate Integration Challenges

As new tools emerge, integrating them with existing systems can be a challenge. Developing problem-solving skills in this area can be valuable.

Example: The API Integration Specialist

A software developer who specialized in API integrations became invaluable to her company as they adopted new communication tools. Her ability to seamlessly connect new platforms with existing systems made technology transitions much smoother for the entire organization.

As we prepare for the next wave of digital communication tools, remember that the goal is not to adopt every new technology, but to thoughtfully select and integrate tools that enhance our ability to connect, collaborate, and communicate effectively. By staying curious, adaptable, and grounded in fundamental communication skills, we can navigate the exciting future of digital communication with confidence and success.

Conclusion

Stepping into the vibrant world of future communication might seem daunting, especially for those who've long found comfort in the quieter corners of social interaction. But remember, dear reader, that every voice, even the softest whisper, has the power to shape our collective future.

To you, the introspective thinker, the careful observer, the one who's often felt overshadowed in a world that seems to reward the loudest voices: your time has come. The communication landscape we've explored isn't just evolving; it's diversifying, creating spaces where every personality can thrive.

Imagine a future where your thoughtful insights can be shared without the pressure of immediate face-to-face interaction. Picture a world where technology amplifies your unique perspective, allowing it to reach those who need to hear it most. The tools and trends we've discussed aren't just advancements, they're invitations. Invitations for you to step forward, to share your voice in ways that feel authentic and comfortable.

Your natural inclination for reflection, your ability to listen deeply, and your capacity for meaningful one-on-one connections are superpowers in this new era of communication. As we move towards more immersive and personalized interactions, your skills will become increasingly valuable.

So, to the shy, the reserved, the quietly powerful: the future of communication isn't just knocking at your door, it's opening up a whole new world of possibilities. It's offering you tools tailored to your strengths, platforms that value depth over volume, and opportunities to connect on your own terms.

Take that first step. Embrace the changes that resonate with you. Your voice, your thoughts, and your presence matter more than you realize. The world of tomorrow needs your unique perspective, and these emerging tools are here to help you share it.

As we close this book, remember: the future of communication isn't just for the bold and the loud. It's for you, too. It's a future that's richer, more nuanced, and more inclusive because you're a part of it. So come, step out of your shell at your own pace, in your own way. The world is ready to listen to what you have to say.